Fragments from a Life

a memoir

John Litchen

Fragments from a Life

a memoir

John Litchen

Yambu

Ist published as a limited edition for private circulation
in 1996 as Fragments from a Life. © J Litchen 1996.

A small segment of this work was previously published as
The Day of Arrival, in Australian Writer Oct/Nov 1994.

Translated into Greek by Chris Andalis in 2007 as
Thripsala Tis Zois, © Chris Andalis 2007.

*Agelidis Foundation Ist Prize winner for unpublished book
length manuscipt in Greek Language 2007.*

Published simultaneously in Greek and English
© J Litchen 2009.
Second printing ©2015

English ISBN: 978-0-9804104-1-9
Greek ISBN: 978-0-9804104-2-6

National Library of Australia Catalogue-in-Publication entry
Litchen, John.
Fragments from a life / John Litchen.
1st Edition.
9780980410419 (pbk.)
Litchen, Spiro, 1898-1989.
Greeks--Australia--Biography
Immigrants--Australia--Biography.
920.009289

Published by; Yambu
PO Box 3503, Robina Town Centre Qld 4230.
Contact: John Litchen. 07 5578 8748, jlitchen@bigpond.net.au

In memory of
SPIROS KIRIAKOU LITSIS
1898-1989

Spiro Litchen in 1924

Dedicated to my brothers and sisters Zara, Phillip, Christine and
Paul, and to Mum who sadly is no longer with us,
and to our older sister Verga who also is no longer with us.
Without your collective memories and the small notebooks
left to us by Dad this story would never have been told.

"I always thought it was much bigger", the old man said in his faded voice when he came home.

Seventy years ago when he had left for the New World his village of Dervitsani had been alive. Every evening people promenaded along its main street, stopping here and there to gossip with friends, taking time to sit in a kafeneion to drink a glass of Ouzo, or to savour a tiny cup of Turkish coffee accompanied by a large glass of the deliciously clean water which they would sip to cleanse the palate.

Young men were often seen teasing groups of girls who turned away blushing and giggling amongst themselves. Seeing this, older women dressed head to feet in black, scolded the boys, telling them to leave the girls alone or they would put the evil eye on them.

The boys would run down the street laughing.

Who listened to the threats of old women?

There was music too; tambours, and violins and clarinets, playing wonderful Epirotic music that lifted one's soul higher than the mountain tops. And wherever there was music there was dancing, with lines of men, their arms across each other's shoulders dancing in unison, always led by some high spirited young man who liked to show off.

But that was seventy years ago. Now the village was deserted and dilapidated, almost a ghost town, and the only sound echoing along the main street was the harsh sighing of cold winds that blew down off the mountains.

He stood in the middle of the main street and he might as well have been standing in a creek bed.

The road that once had a bitumen surface was nothing more than a gravel track cut with deep furrows. Scattered along it as far as he could see were pebbles worn smooth by running water that came from rain dumped onto the village by the furious storms that often fell off the mountain tops to lash the valleys below in spring and the lead up to winter. Huge rocks stuck up randomly as if they had been thrust out of the ground by a giant hand. Tufts of grass grew in the little mounds of soil that gathered behind them. Vehicles using this remnant of a road had to weave a zig-zag pattern along it to avoid those rocks.

An old woman dressed in ragged black clothes with a scarf covering her head sidled past. She threw a furtive glance in his direction before disappearing into a shadow filled gap between two houses.

A couple of men walked slowly along the other side of the street from where the old man stood. They were probably not anywhere near the age of the old man but they might as well have been. Their faces were as damaged and as worn away as the main street. Neither of them spoke to each other. They looked neither left nor right but only down towards the ground ahead of them as they shuffled along.

The old man turned and walked hesitantly past the last of the houses. He had walked the length of the main street staring at the houses of rock and earth. They were so small, the cracked doorways so narrow, the windows so tiny and grimy, that he found it hard to believe he used to live in one of them.

Tears welled up in his eyes as he walked past the end of the last row of houses near the edge of the village because he could not remember which house was the one he had grown up in.

***

When I was a small boy there were twelve of us in our family, all living together in the one house.

It was a house of two rooms and a kitchen. My father had four children and my uncle, two. Grandfather and grandmother slept together with my uncle and aunt and my two cousins in one room while Mum and Dad, my two brothers, myself and my sister all used the other room. We were quite happy as long as we had enough to eat. We had no beds, but we had plenty of blankets and we were used to sleeping on the floor. We didn't know any different.

There weren't too many chairs either. All of us kids sat cross-legged on the floor, and at night we used oil lamps to see with since there was no electricity.

We had about ten acres of rocky land, which we didn't own but rented from the Turkish overlords. Ten or fifteen percent of whatever we produced was what they got. We grew wheat, barley and oats, rock melons, okra, and onions. We had two oxen, a couple of cows and a pig.

We made bread from the wheat, the barley and oats fed the cows, and the melons, okra and onions we used to sell. Dad was the only one who didn't work the land.

He was a school teacher.

***

The land around his village had always been hard and rocky, with mountains cut sharp in the thin air. Small scattered hollows filled with soil were cherished by various families who managed to grow meagre crops of vegetables during the warm spring and summer months. Tiny flocks of sheep were grazed on the high mountain plains, each guarded zealously by a flinty eyed shepherd. There were many starving bandits who were only too happy to steal a sheep because they also had families to feed.

In 1898, when the old man was born, his village was under control of the Ottoman Empire, and taxes in the form of goods were paid to the local Pasha by all of the families living there. If there was anything left over after this tribute had been paid, the people could keep it, but since the soil was so poor there was often nothing left over. Many would go hungry for a time, surviving only through the kindness of others who were willing to share what little extra they had.

Anyone old enough left the village in search of work.

They rarely came back.

***

In 1913 politics intervened when the big European Powers were frightened that Greece and Serbia, along with Montenegro and Bulgaria with their newly founded Balkan League might become too powerful, stepped in and delineated where the borders of each country should be. They broke up the countries and created Albania from territories belonging to Serbia, Macedonia and Greece which were added to the tiny tribal area that the Albanians originally occupied. Naturally those Albanians were happy, but all the others belonging to the annexed areas were upset, furious, even rebellious, but there was nothing anyone could do about it. Greece lost a good part of Northern Epirus and overnight the old man's village found itself to be a part of Albania instead of Greece. The people were told they were Albanians.

The border was closed, with every known crossing guarded, and the people from all those villages close to the new border with Greece were forbidden to visit friends and relatives only a few kilometres away.

At school their children were forced to learn the Albanian language. No official business in the village, or any other of the villages that had been annexed, would be conducted in Greek or Serbian or Macedonian, only Albanian was to be used.

***

While we looked after the melons, my mother and aunt, and my sister, like most of the other women in the village, scoured the hills for kindling. It was needed to start fires in the winter. If the men couldn't gather enough heavy wood during the summer, then it was the women's job to prepare dung for fuel.

No one in our village could afford to buy coal so they used horse and cow dung. The women would soften it with water then mix in finely chopped chaff or dry grass. Some of them would mould this mixture into bricks which they would leave stacked by the side of the house to dry in the sun. Others would make flat round cakes which they slapped onto the walls underneath the eaves where it would stick and stay dry even when the weather was bad. My mother did it this way.

In the winter she would chip it off the walls and bring it inside where it would be broken into smaller bits and fed into the fire. She kept the fire burning continuously during the harsh winter months. I can remember, no matter how cold and icy it got outside, even when it was cold enough for the ground to freeze, it was always warm and cosy inside our house.

5

***

I was ten or almost ten when my older brother George went to America. My sister was married off to a man from another village and she moved there to live. My other brother, Christos, who was also older than me, had also gone to America. He did not like it there and returned after only a few months. He turned up unexpectedly after crossing the mountains from Greece, surprising everyone because we all thought he was still in America. He didn't say why he came back but I think he preferred the solitude of the mountains. Being a shepherd, he had missed his sheep, and the wild rugged beauty of the Epirotic Mountains.

That's what he told me when I was older, but in retrospect he probably missed the excitement of smuggling things over the border from Greece. He was one of those who knew the secret ways through the mountains down into Greece.

His excuse for being in the mountains if questioned by Albanian or Turkish speaking soldiers was that he was a shepherd. Sometimes a sheep went astray and he had to look for it.

"No one can afford to lose a sheep," he would tell them while smiling politely, "especially when the mountains are full of bandits, only too ready to grab anything that they think might be useful."

***

The old man would tell us sometimes how he had helped Christos to guard the sheep.

He might have been eleven or twelve at the time.

All he could really remember though was how cold it was in those high mountain passes with the wind slipping down off the snow.

"I could never get my hands warm," he said. "No one in our family had gloves, so I used to wrap old bits of cloth around my fingers to keep the chill out of them."

"One night it got so cold my blasted fingers stuck to the metal of the rifle."

He clenched his fingers involuntarily as he remembered.

"If someone had come to steal a sheep then, while Christos was over the mountains arranging to smuggle back things we all needed, I would not have been able to shoot him."

He chuckled at the memory of that rifle.

"It was so obsolete I don't think it would have worked anyway."

***

In 1920, after I had come back from America there were bandits everywhere. They lived in the mountains, and no village was safe.

Italian soldiers had replaced the Turks, after the end of the First World War, but no one thought much of them.

Sometime in 1923 the European Powers formed a provisional Albanian Government, but until they brought King Zog in to run the country things were chaotic.

We were all still upset because our village Dervitsani had ended up in Albania instead of Greece back in 1913. Nothing had changed since then.

The border was only a couple of Kilometres away.

We could easily have been on the Greek side where we belonged. But no matter how the Greek Government protested, the dominant Powers were adamant that the border was where they had marked the line on the maps, and that's where it would stay. They didn't care one bit about whose life was disrupted. It was unimportant to them whether you were Greek or Albanian; they just drew the line and said this side is Greece and that side is Albania.

Can you imagine that?

There were a number of small Greek villages and towns stuck inside Albania, and there was nothing any of us living there could do about it. The border was closed. No one was allowed across it from either side. Most likely if you were seen attempting to cross it you would be shot by the soldiers guarding the border. So naturally people familiar with the area found many secret ways through the mountains which avoided the manned crossing points.

We were also easy prey for the bandits that ran wild in the hills. They were Albanian, not Greek, and their religion was Muslim, and not Greek Orthodox. They would sneak down out of the mountains and steal whatever they could get their hands on. Sheep, cows, bags of wheat: anything of value. If anyone protested the bandits would beat them until they were black and blue.

Sometimes they even shot them.

Occasionally they would kidnap someone from a village and

hold him for ransom. It usually wasn't much, but the villagers had to chip in to pay it, and that was hard when none of us ever had much to begin with.

I used to think we were better off under the Turks, than the Albanians. At least you knew where you stood with them.

Finally we got sick of this constant pilfering so a few men went over the mountains into Greece where they got some rifles and ammunition.

Christos was one of those who had helped organise the guns. He led the party over the border to bring them back. How they got them Christos would not say, but I do believe the Greek Army had something to do with it. They were forbidden to come across the border to reclaim Greek territory, but the least they could do was help Greeks over there fight off Albanian bandits by supplying the villages with weapons.

Once we got the guns we had no trouble with bandits. We all took turns patrolling the village day and night, but especially at night.

Word soon got around that we were armed and that anyone trying to steal from us would get shot.

***

Every summer when the melons started growing, my Grandfather would build a hut where he would stay to guard them. He would take our oxen and go into the forest where he would cut a load of tree branches. The oxen would carry the loads back to the melon field.

He was good at building huts, and would have it constructed in one day. The roof and walls he would make from bull rushes from the creek at the bottom of the valley.

We boys would go there and look after the hut during the summer school holidays. Of course we also had to look after the melons as there were lots of thieves and bandits in the mountains who would have loved to steal our melons, not to mention neighbours' cows and horses which were partial to a bit of fresh melon. We had lots of fun chasing the cows away.

We loved it up there, on our own, because it made us feel important and grown up.

***

The day after I turned twelve my father organised an apprenticeship for me with a tailor he knew who lived in a nearby village.

There was no more school for me. Six years was all any of the children in our village did. There were no higher schools and no one could afford to send their children to other towns or cities where they could get a better education. We all had to work.

I was happy about the apprenticeship. Tailoring was a good trade. But it was hard not being able to live at home. I missed everyone, and although the tailor was a kind man I felt very lonely for the first year. I used to walk home every Sunday even though it took a couple of hours so I could have Sunday dinner with my family.

That first year was really tough. I used to sit cross legged on the floor with my fingers tied back so I would get used to the correct way of sewing.

You can't imagine how my fingers used to ache. These days, with machines, sewing is easy, but we had to do it all by hand, and that was time consuming. You had to have good eyes and a steady hand.

The first thing the tailor did was to place a thimble on my middle finger, and then this was bent forward and tied in position so I couldn't move it. You hold the needle with the thumb and the index finger and you push it through the material with the side of the thimble. The end of the thimble has a hole in it and the needle would get stuck in there or in your finger if you used that part, so you always push the needle with the side of the thimble. Once you get used to this sideways movement you can sew very fast.

The first thing I was taught was to over lock the stitch, the way modern machines do it. I had to learn to do this by hand and it took almost three months before I could make absolutely straight lines of stitching. Once I could do that I started on buttonholes — trouser button holes, which are of course hidden so it doesn't matter if you make them a bit rough at first. There were no such things as zips in those days.

By the time I started on buttonholes the tailor allowed me to sew without my fingers being tied back. Whenever I sat down to sew my fingers would automatically curl into the right position.

Then I learnt how to do button holes in waistcoats, and finally sac coats, which were the hardest.

For these I had to use two needles: one in the left hand which carried a cord around the buttonhole, while the right hand holding the other needle and thimble did the fine stitching. And it had to be very fine and neat too because this was the first thing anyone would see when they looked at a coat.

It took me another three months to learn how to do good button holes. After that, the rest of my time was spent learning how to measure and cut, and how to fit and alter suits that weren't quite right.

After a year, I could measure, cut, sew, and fit a suit. To take a piece of material and turn it into a fine looking suit was something I enjoyed immensely. By the end of my two year apprenticeship, I was a fully qualified tailor, and could make a suit then as good as any suit you can buy now in a shop.

***

Many young men left the village, even those who were married. They went to America, to Argentina, and to Australia.

Since my two brothers had done it – gone to America – although they had come back a couple of years later, there was in the back of my mind the thought that I should probably do that too. Of course I felt I was too young, but I was a tailor and would be able to get work, so perhaps age didn't matter too much.

In these far away places, alien lands where other languages were spoken, we heard tales that as strangers the men from our village and others nearby were sometimes despised, but these men persevered and for a while they sent money back so their families could be better off.

Sometimes they sent for their wives and children.

Sometimes the money stopped coming and no one ever knew what had happened because the letters from those people also stopped coming.

At those times there was sadness and bitterness in the village, and with all but the oldest men leaving, there were only the mothers and the sisters and the smallest children left.

***

Halley's Comet as seen on 29th - March 1910.
Published in the New York Times July 3 1910.

"I remember Halley's Comet," the old man said on the night we went to look at the fuzzy ball barely visible in the dust shrouded sky not far from Melbourne.

He must have been twelve or thirteen when the comet arrived.

"It was much closer that time," he said. "Every night for months it was in the sky — right across the sky with a long burning tail. Not a fuzzy ball like that." He pointed into the night sky where the vague ball shape of the comet was barely discernable.

We were too close to Melbourne for clear viewing, what with light pollution from the city and no doubt considerable industrial pollution filling the air with dust and smoke and ozone. Even with a super clear sky the comet would not have been very spectacular.

"We could hear it hissing and we could smell the sulphur in the air. Everybody was terrified."

"Come on," we said. "Nobody could hear it hissing. No matter how close it looked it still would have been millions of miles out in space. There would have been no smell. It was all in your imagination."

But he was adamant. He had smelt the sulphur, he had heard the comet hissing in the sky; they all had.

"Go and ask them, they'll all tell you the same thing."

But there was no one we could ask. One by one over the years his compatriots, those other men from his village, had all died.

He was the only one left.

Perhaps the sulphur in the air was nothing more than the smell of gunpowder from distant battles in nearby provinces, and what he had heard was only the wind whistling around the barren rocks in the mountains that straddle the border between Greece and Albania, his youthful imagination endowing that soft sibilant sound with a mystical quality.

It was the year the Turks would finally be kicked out of Epirus. His world was coming to an end, his life was about to change, and comets, especially Halley's, the greatest of them all, were seen as harbingers of destruction.

***

During the year of the comet the Turks were nervous and skittish. There was rebellion in the air, and many young men in the villages of Northern Epirus were being conscripted into the armies of the Pasha.

The Greeks had joined with Serbia, Montenegro and Bulgaria to form the Balkan League. They were determined to push their Turkish Overlords back into Turkey to regain possession and sovereignty of their own countries. After four hundred and eighty years of domination they wanted to be free. We all wanted to be free.

In our village, the older boys ran off to hide in the mountains when the Turkish soldiers came looking for recruits. None of us wanted to fight for the Turkish side against our own people.

One night, after the Turks had left, my brother George said to me: "We should go to America before the war starts."

***

Seeing on television the thousands of refugees from Albania refusing to leave Italy where they had sought refuge, refusing to go back to what could be death, refusing to be bribed by the offers of more clothes and new shoes, brought to mind those other Albanians and Greeks who left for similar and compelling reasons almost one hundred years ago. The stark image of one scrawny man claiming that to die a free man in Italy was better than being sent back to Albania should stay in everyone's mind for ever.

***

My oldest brother George had returned from America with glowing tales of the prospects available. This naturally inspired all the young men, and even young teenagers like myself. We all wanted to go there.

But the Turks wouldn't allow anyone to leave. They were conscripting all the young men to fight in the their army. They were terrified that the Greeks and the allied Balkans were going to push them out.

When the Turks came looking for conscripts in our village, my brother George and I decided to leave.

Like many other young men in the Greek villages of North Epirus, we refused to be on the Turkish side fighting against our own people. Christos had disappeared into the mountains with his sheep. Others headed off into the mountains attempting to cross over into Greece where they preferred to join the Greek army.

We joined a small group who were going to make their way down to the coast where we could somehow sneak across the water to the island of Kerkyra which although directly opposite Albania was Greek territory.

It was a bitterly cold night when we left.

Frozen stars glistened as bright as the tears on our mother's face. All we had was what we were wearing, and my mother would not let go of me. I suppose it was because I was the last of her children and she thought she would never see me again.

"Come on Zaharo, let him go," my father said. "He won't stay in America all his life; he'll be back one day."

I'm sure she only let me go because I was travelling with my older brother.

***

He always used to cry when any of us went away on a long trip or a holiday. We would tease him about it, about how emotional he was. He would simply turn away and wipe the tears from his eyes, then turn back with a smile, as if nothing had happened.

It would be many years before any of us could comprehend the reason for those tears.

***

"I'll never forget the tears in my mother's eyes when she let me go," the old man said quietly one day. "She never did say good bye."

***

The Balkan League did so well pushing the Turks back in 1913 that the big European Powers started to worry about what could happen in the rest of Europe. Fearful that the largest two members of the League, Greece and Serbia, would become too powerful, they stepped in to forestall this possibility.

They made Albania bigger, the old man said, by taking some of the territories belonging to both Greece and Serbia. So Greece lost control of part of North Epirus, and those Greeks living there were told once again they were now Albanians. They did not like it one bit, but there was nothing they could do about it.

Bulgaria didn't like either. They figured Greece and Serbia got the best deal so they so they turned on their neighbours and attacked them. They too wanted a larger share of the spoils, but they could not beat Greece and Serbia combined so they were pushed back towards Turkey, and both Greece and Serbia regained their respective parts of Macedonia. And that's how the first Balkan war ended. That was in 1913, not long after that we left for America.

***

I don't remember the ride down the mountains on the back of that wagon, except that it was pulled by two horses. Once we got to Ksamil the others in our group dispersed. They had arrangments with different fishermen who were to take them across to Kerkyra.

A lot of fishermen were only too happy to act as ferrymen for those wanting to escape Albania. They hardly got paid anything for the fish they caught and the little extra money the refugees gave them was a bonus. In any case the refugees had no use for their money in Greece. The Greeks wouldn't accept Albanian money under any circumstances.

We hid in the hut of a fisherman who was a friend of our father until it got dark, and then he took us a couple of kilometres down the coast from Ksamil to a secluded beach where another fisherman with a dinghy waited.

I had never seen the sea before and I was terrified. It looked like an upside down sky that kept heaving and moving. Fortunately when we left it was dark and I couldn't see how much water there really was.

"I don't know how to swim" I told the fisherman as he helped me into his little boat. I had trouble getting in because the boat kept moving up and down and shifting sideways.

"We have to be silent so no one can hear us," the fisherman said, once George and I were settled in the middle of the boat. He started to row quietly out into the sea.

I had this awful feeling in my stomach as the dinghy moved up and down.

***

The noise of the sail slapping and filling with wind shattered the silence of the night.

"We are in Greek territory," the fisherman shouted triumphantly as he steered the dinghy towards the dark bulk of the island of Kerkyra.

I couldn't wait to get ashore. We were only three kilometres away from Albania, and already it felt as if we were in another world.

The sea air had a different and sweetly seductive smell, so unlike the dry harsh air in the mountains we had left behind.

***

Kerkyra was Saint Spyridon's island. And for me it was like stepping into a world of freedom. I had been christened on Saint Spyridon's day and was given his name, Spiros. I was also given the name Kiriakou after my father so everyone would know to which family I belonged. They would have known anyway, since everyone in the village knew everyone else.

I felt this immense sense of belonging the moment I stepped on the shore of Kerkyra.

'The Turks had never managed to conquer this island,' my father had told me.

Spyridon was a third century bishop who once lived in Cyprus. His corpse had been taken and carried away to escape desecration by the advancing Turks. It eventually found a place of rest on the island of Kerkyra, forever safe from Turkish incursions.

They told me he emerges four times a year to lead a procession that celebrates his miraculous intervention during times of famine, epidemics, and siege.

Unfortunately I never saw one of those processions. We weren't there long enough.

After staring back at the black shadow that was the coast of Albania across the water I was glad to have left. We had landed at a fairly remote place and walked for hours until we found someone to direct us to a town. Once there we went to the police station. It was still early in the morning and we had to wait for them to open, but once the policemen arrived we told them we had escaped from Albania.

They welcomed us to Greece as if we were long lost brothers, then they took us to the Epirotic Society and the people there arranged for us to get Greek passports stating that we were citizens of Corfu, or Kerkyra.

***

We travelled on an Italian ship to Brindisi where we were quarantined for a several days.

The voyage across had been smooth with the sea calm as a giant lake. Inside the ship it felt smooth and I found it hard to believe we were actually travelling across water, but once ashore it was a different matter entirely.

"It was disgusting, the way they treated us," the old man said. "We were all immigrating to America and the first thing they did was to make us take all our clothes off and get into a shower together. Youths and adults, we had to wash each other down, scrub each other with a foul smelling soap, then they turned huge hoses on us and washed it all off."

We have different customs in Epirus.

We never did things like that.

***

When we got to America, New York it was, the ship docked at an island in the middle of the harbour. I could see the statue of Liberty on another little island very close to us and thought how wonderful she looked. I had never seen any statue as big as that before. Everyone wanted to look at the statue or the skyline of the great city of New York across the water.

We had arrived. This was America, the place everyone dreamed about. Would any of our dreams come true?

Before any of us got too excited they herded us off the ship and into this huge room where there were rows and rows of people. They pushed us around like animals, prodding and shoving us to keep us moving. There was so much noise and confusion I couldn't understand a word they said.

I was so sick. I had been sea sick all the way across the Atlantic. I felt so weak I could hardly stand up. My brother George was helping me to stand when some official came and said something to him about me. My brother shook his head, but the official only smiled. He took me away and they stuck me in a room that was all white. There was a bed they made me get into.

It was so good to lay down on something that did not move all the time.

***

There are mountains out there in the Atlantic. Huge mountains of water, and the ship went up and down them with a lot of shuddering and noise. It rocked from side to side and sometimes it felt like it slipped down the sideways stopping suddenly when it hit the bottom and huge amounts of water would slosh over the decks before the ship would shake like a dog trying to flick the water off.

Then the engines would grind and groan as the ship pushed itself up the side of another mountain of water.

We travelled in steerage and the smell down there was horrible. Almost everyone was sick. I was so sick I could not eat anything at all. I could not even drink water without vomiting it back up.

When we got to America because I looked so wasted away they thought I had Tuberculosis, and put me in quarantine. If I did have Tuberculosis, they told George, they would send me back.

It was a week before they realised I had only been seasick and dehydrated. After giving me lots of fluid and some medicine as well as some awful food, they let my brother come and get me.

I went back through immigration, and I was given a new family name because they couldn't pronounce my original one.

But that didn't worry me. I was in America, that's all that mattered.

I was no longer frightened they were going to send me back. I would never have survived the trip back.

They asked what work I could do, and I remembered George said that I had to tell them, "I will do anything."

They smiled and one of them stamped my passport.

"You'll do fine," he said.

Of course I didn't know what they said, because I knew not a word of English, but George was with me and he translated for me.

***

I could not believe New York was so big.

There were more people in this one city than there were in the whole of Epirus, and the way they rushed around was incredible. There were so many motor carriages, automobiles and trucks.

I had never seen an automobile before. Not even the mayor of our village had one. I couldn't stop staring as George took me to the station where we got a train to Boston. I had never been on a train before either, and at first it was unsettling, but I quickly got used to it.

While I had been in quarantine George arranged to get his old job back, the job in a tanning house in Boston and as soon as we got there I found a job as a tailor in a clothing factory.

It was the day after I had arrived, actually the day after they had allowed me to leave quarantine, and I was already working!

They paid me $9 a week. A man's wage!

Here was I a boy not yet fifteen and earning a man's wage. I couldn't get over it. What would I do with so much money?

I would save it. I would go home a rich man, and marry the best looking girl in the village.

That's what I would do.

***

Unfortunately that job didn't last long.

One day I had an argument with the foreman in the factory. He said I was too slow making a vest.

"You told me," I said to him, "that I could take as long as I want providing I did a good job."

I threw the vest at him and demanded that he look at it.

"Look at the workmanship. Can you do as good as that?"

No one made vests as good as I did.

"I'll time you, and we'll see how long it takes you to make one like that. I'll bet you can't do it."

My English was pretty good by this time. I was going to night school and studying hard.

The foreman was Italian, and we just didn't get on. He was always at me about something, and this business about taking too long to make a vest was the last straw.

The foreman threw his arms up in the air and stormed off. I went and told the boss, who told me not to worry. The foreman was leaving to go back to Italy in the near future.

But the foreman didn't go.

I got the sack instead.

***

I couldn't get another tailoring job anywhere. Lots of people were out of work and it seemed to be getting worse.

The only related job I could get was as a presser in a shirt factory. I worked for Pelaco.

You remember them. For years they had a picture of a black man assisting a white man try on a shirt. The words at the bottom of the picture were: 'Mine tinket it fit.'

I hated that ad, and I didn't like the job much either, but it was all I could get so I stuck it out.

They did make nice shirts though.

***

During the winter there was a black man, an African American who roasted chestnuts on a hotplate that was really the top of a 44 gallon drum.

He had put a grid half way down the drum by hammering some metal bars through it. A rectangular section above the grid had been cut out and made into a flap through which he could put the wood he burnt and a number of holes punched through the bottom of the barrel allowed air to circulate to fan the fire. A small smokestack was bolted to a hole just beneath the hotplate to allow the smoke to get out.

I loved the chestnuts and often bought some. I could never get the man to say much though apart from an abrupt "How many do you want?" and "That'll be a dime."

But one day as I watched him throw a handful of chestnuts onto the hot plate he asked: "Where you from?"

"I'm from Epirus, in Northern Greece," I told him.

"I'm from Africa," he said proudly as he turned the chestnuts over with a small flat piece of iron so they wouldn't burn.

"I like your coat," he said.

"I made it myself last summer. I'm a Tailor."

His coat was old and grey and looked like it was a leftover from the Crimean war. The cuffs were frayed and the elbows were threadbare. It had seen a lot of wear.

"And I'm a Bum," he said. "I can't make nothing, got no trade. All I can do is cook chestnuts. At least it keeps me warm in the winter."

He handed me a bag of hot chestnuts and I paid him a dime.

"One day I'll go to Africa where it's always nice and warm."

He said warm with a deep resonant voice full of longing.

"I've never been there. I was born right here in this city full of cold wind and snow. My Grand Pappy though, he was real African, a slave. He was taken to Cuba by the Spanish then sold to a family in Alabama for breeding stock. That would be a life, huh. I wish someone would use me for breeding stock." He laughed.

"My people were slaves too," I told him.

"No kidding. I never knew white people were slaves."

"The Turks controlled my country for five hundred years. Every thing we produced went to them. All our land belonged to them. Still belongs to them, but some of us escaped and came here where we can be free. But it won't be long and I'll be able to go home. The Turks are finally being pushed back to their own country. Soon we'll all be free."

"I'll drink to that," the black man said. He pulled a flat bottle from his side pocket and uncorked it. "You want some?"

He held it towards me.

"Thank you, but no. I've got to go," I said.

"See you around," he said before taking a snort from the bottle.

I never did see him again. His 44 gallon drum was there in the usual spot, but it had been appropriated by another group of black people who were not the least bit friendly when I asked about him.

"Don't know," the man tending the chestnuts snarled at me as if asking him about the other man was something disagreeable. "You want some chestnuts?"

I decided not to buy any. I didn't like his attitude.

Maybe the other man went to Africa where it was warm all the time, I thought as I walked along the slippery sidewalk where the night's snow had been pushed off and left piled up in the gutter.

***

George also hated the job in the tannery and decided one day he'd had enough.

He and some of the other Greeks about his age decided they were going to go back to Greece. They had the money for the fare. I wanted to go too, but they said I was too young. They were going back, they said, to join the Greek army so they could fight against the Turks, to help push them all the way back to Turkey.

The European powers had given Greece permission to occupy Smyrna, which was in Asia Minor. Almost two million Greeks were living in Asia Minor still under the rule of the Ottoman Empire. As the First World War ended the Allies accepted the surrender of Bulgaria and agreed to an armistice with Turkey and were marching on Constantinople. Greece wanted control of the territories in Asia Minor once occupied by the Byzantine Empire.

The Big Powers were happy to let the Greek army lead the way as they would take the worst of whatever the Turks could throw at them.

Instead of frightening the Turks, as the Greeks thought they would, the resistance of the Turks solidified and they fought back ferociously. The Greeks were tired and overextended, while the Turks under the leadership of Mustapha Kemal, known to the world as Ataturk, slaughtered the Greeks.

Fifty thousand were killed before the second war in the Balkans was over.

***

George and his compatriots were still on the ship going to Greece when news that the Turks had slaughtered 50,000 Greek soldiers in Anatolia was broadcast on the radio and published in major newspapers all through America, and no doubt the whole world.

Giant headlines announced how many had been slaughtered. There were pictures of dead soldiers, Evzones, with their pleated skirts covered in blood and dirt, their white stockinged legs broken and twisted, on the front pages of all the newspapers.

I was glad George had not got back in time to be a part of that massacre.

***

I was tired of pressing shirts even though the pay was good. I had enough money saved to go home, maybe even enough to buy a house. My longing to go strengthened day by day. America was an exciting place, but I missed the tranquillity of the mountains and valleys around my hometown. I missed my parents and all the people I knew. I missed the sound of Greek voices in the streets and cafes. With George gone there was no one close to me here. I really was alone. It was time to go home.

I spoke to a couple of friends, not people from my village but other Epirotics, and told them of my plans. They decided to do the same, so we quit our jobs and took the first train to New York.

All the ships going to Europe went from New York.

***

With the First World War over, New York was crazy. There were so many people trying to go back to Europe that the queues in front of the various embassies stretched for blocks. People were camping in the queues so they wouldn't loose their places. If any-one tried to push in, to jump the queue, they would be thrown back into the street; maybe even beaten up. Police patrolled the queues so there would not be too much violence.

When we saw the queue stretching away from the immigration department where we had to go first for our exit permits my friends and I were dismayed. It seemed to stretch for miles.

As we walked along the queue we discovered there were many Greeks like us who had decided to go back. Some had been many years in America. Others like me had only been here six or seven years.

"Go to the end of the queue," we were told time and time again.

"Have you brought some food?"

"You'll be days in the queue."

There was a policeman walking along ahead of us no doubt keeping an eye on possible troublemakers. I hurried along to catch him and asked: "Why is the queue moving so slow?"

He turned and glared at me for a moment but then realising I had spoken to him in good English he said, "Because hardly any of these people can speak English, and that slows down the processing."

"I see," I muttered as an idea occurred to me. I hurried back to my two friends.

"Give me your passports," I said. "I've got an idea."

***

"Where do you think you're going?" the guard at the main entrance to the Immigration building asked.

"Official business," I stated in my best English. "I'm the translator."

He looked dubiously at me for a few seconds, and I could see he wasn't sure whether to believe me or not. So before he could make up his mind one way or the other, I said, "Are you going to tell me where I have to go, or am I supposed to go in there and find out by myself?"

Immediately he opened the door and signalled for another guard to come over to escort me to the officer in charge of the Exit Visa applications.

I explained to this gentleman that I had come to offer my services as a translator for those Greeks wanting to leave the country, if he would in turn stamp mine and my friend's passports so that we would be able to catch our ship in time.

He laughed. "You're okay," he said. "Give me the passports,

and go and get one of those chairs over there."

I got the chair and sat next to him. He gave me back the passports with the exit visas stamped and dated, and said: "Now let's get to work. We'll do the Greek ones first now that you are here."

I couldn't imagine the consternation that would cause amongst the many hundreds lined up outside, down the street and around the block– not all of them were Greek – but I didn't care. I had my visa, and my friends had theirs.

And tomorrow morning we would be on our way home.

***

"If I get airsick I'm getting off in Sydney," the old man said unequivocally. "I'll come back by train."

"You won't get airsick," we assured him. "The Jumbo jet is much smoother than any other planes you've ever been in. You won't even know you're in the air."

"The last time I went somewhere in a plane I got airsick."

"That was in 1925."

"I went to Mildura, and I haven't been in a plane since."

"We know. You've told us a million times. There's been a lot of improvement over the last fifty years."

"All right," he said after a long pause. He knew as well as we did that if he wanted to go overseas he would have to fly. There was no way he would ever go by ship.

"But if I get sick I'm getting off in Sydney," he said stubbornly so as not to lose face. "I'll come back by train."

"Okay, it's a deal."

"Good, then I'll give it a try."

***

One week after leaving New York the French ship we were travelling on got into some very rough weather. I was of course travelling steerage again, but it was not as bad as the Italian ship I came across to America on. There were only fifteen bunks in this cabin, not fifty. We weren't far from the kitchen and every time the ship heaved I could hear plates crashing onto the fl oor. We had to hang on to the sides of the bunk so as not to be hurled onto the floor like the plates.

Of course I got sea sick again. I was so dizzy I could hardly walk and had to be helped by my two compatriots when we went up on deck to be vaccinated before entering French waters. The medical orderly shoved me forward when it was my turn, saying in French: 'move along pig.'

French had been one of my best subjects at school and I had no trouble understanding what he had said. I turned back and told him in French he was the pig if that was the way he treated people. After that he kept quiet as the ship's doctor vaccinated my group against smallpox.

I didn't like the French much. Their attitude to foreigners was always one of arrogance and disdain, even in Marseilles, where you would think they were used to people from other countries.

While looking for somewhere to stay for a few days I passed a butcher shop not far from the Port where we had disembarked. It had the usual meats one would expect to see in butcher's shop but there were two huge horse's heads hanging from large hooks in the middle of the window.

I couldn't believe it.

Staring at those heads on display my feelings that the French were refined vanished forever.

I didn't know they ate horses.

***

After two weeks in Marseilles we managed to get passage aboard an English hospital ship going to Saloniki in Greece. The ship carried wounded soldiers. This ship had only one class and the waiters and crew were all very friendly and polite.

One of the stewards even brought me my breakfast in bed when I was feeling dizzy and couldn't get up. They never did that on the Italian or French ships.

It was November 1919, almost the start of winter but the weather was very good. The sea was calm and I spent most of the day on deck. A group of sailors were playing Irish and Scottish dances which I liked very much. They had such a happy feel to them. When they stopped playing they chatted and joked in a language I couldn't understand. I asked the waiter who had brought me my breakfast in bed what language they were talking and he said English.

"I don't believe it," I said.

"They speak a different dialect in the North," he explained.

"Can you understand them?"

"Of course, no one in England would have any trouble understanding them, or you" he told me. "You speak like an American. But people in different parts of England have very different accents; they don't all speak the same kind of English as I do. You might have trouble understanding them."

I was sure I would. No matter how carefully I listened I could not decipher one word they said.

But the music was good. I loved the music.

***

And there was music in Saloniki too: joyous happy music.

Everywhere I walked people played music. It emanated from every restaurant, from every taverna; even from the open windows of private houses.

Though the city looked as if an earthquake had struck it, with most buildings apart from the town hall damaged in some way, the feeling that filled the city was of infectious joy.

I was so excited I felt like dancing as I walked on Greek soil for the first time in years. I would have knelt down and kissed the ground, but the thought of doing this suddenly made me self conscious.

But I wasn't home yet.

I still had mountains to cross, and a border manned by Italian troops to negotiate.

***

From the bus to Ioannina I stared in awe at the monasteries perched precariously on the tops of the mountains near Meteora.

They were built by monks who lived in the caves on top of these strange mountains during the fourteenth century. They had wanted to contemplate the word of God in a little more comfort while remaining in isolation from the rest of the world so they built these unbelievable structures out of the rock found on the mountains.

More isolated you could not get, I thought when I saw that the only access to these monasteries was by a wobbling wicker basket lowered down or pulled up from far above.

***

It was dawn when we arrived in Ioannina and the part of town down near the lake was shrouded in mist rising up off the icy water. All we could see was the black shadow of the mountains on the other side far across the lake. The water was so still I couldn't tell where the surface was and where the mist began. The mist was reflected in such a way that it appeared to be underwater struggling to break through the surface so it could escape into the cold air above. Ali Pasha's Mosque on the island out in the lake was invisible, shrouded by the slowly writhing mist.

I had an eerie feeling looking at the mist on the lake for the first time, and wondered if the stories my father had told me were true. I remember him saying once that the ghosts of the concubines Ali Pasha had drowned came out of the lake with the mist in the mornings.

Ali Pasha had been the conqueror and the ruler of Epirus, and a tyrannical monster he had been too. At the head of his invincible army he had torn Epirus apart.

He took the most beautiful girls for his harem, and at one stage he had, my father said, over 500 concubines. He was even partial to handsome young men and devoted as much time to them as he did to women.

If anyone objected to his advances he would have them killed. Anyone, concubine or male lover who didn't please him was tied hand and foot, weighted with stones, stuffed into a sack, and dropped into the lake.

He would laugh as the sack sank into the icy water. When the rising bubbles stopped he would survey those around him to see if there were any more people who objected to his choice of concubine or his treatment of them.

I stared at the mists and shivered.

It was the cold. That was all.

There were no ghosts out there. But I'll bet there are plenty of bones, I told myself.

***

"Hey," one of my friends called to me. "What are you doing staring at the lake? You can't see anything. You're not looking for ghosts are you?" And he laughed.

"Let's find somewhere where we can get a hot cup of coffee," another said.

Both these two young men had travelled with me all the way from America. They lived in different villages which had been annexed when our part of Epirus was given to the Albanians. They wanted to go home as much as I did.

We walked along the path around the lakefront until we saw a place just opening. It wasn't far from a market place where people were already setting up tables and stalls. The sky was rapidly getting lighter and the mist was disappearing off the lake.

Hot thick sweet coffee and bread rolls straight from the oven. It was beautiful. Nothing I had ever eaten in America had tasted this delicious.

I was content. I was home. Well, almost home. The mist was becoming transparent, vanishing as I watched, and the water of the lake was so still it was like a sheet of glass. There was not a ripple anywhere. Now I could see Ali Pasha's mosque on its little island out in the lake.

I ordered another coffee and was just starting to sip it when in walked the father of one of my second cousins. I couldn't believe it.

When I told him who I was, he stared at me. I think he thought I was trying to trick him. I told him a few things about myself and some things that as a nephew only I would know, and he was finally convinced.

"Have I changed that much that you don't recognise me?"

"You were only a little boy when I last saw you. Maybe nine years old, and now you are a man."

"What are you doing here?" I asked.

"I run a truck over the mountains to Argyrokastro. I bring things to sell at the market. If you want I'll take you home. I go

35

right past your village. Are your papers in order?"

I showed him my passport with its exit visa from America, Greek stamps and so on.

"You should be fine," he said. "The guards on the border are all Italian. They don't care who comes and goes as long as you've got the right stamps on your papers."

The war was over and everybody seemed happy. It would be a good time to arrive home.

***

I was only a boy, barely a teenager, when I had left home, and now I was returning as a young man. Would anyone recognise me?

It was all I could think of as we bounced along the rough roads through the mountains between Greece and Albania.

It was dark and clear with sharp stars and a full moon to light the way. It was very much like the night when my brother and I had left for America years ago. Only this time I wasn't frightened, I was happy. What a difference that made to the night!

***

We were let off by a side road that led down a valley to our village. Not far down the road I could hear voices and saw some flickering lights. There were people by the river fishing. They used the lights to attract the fish, which they caught in traps. My two companions called out and fishermen came over to see who we were.

I recognised them immediately since they had been much older than I when I had left for America. No one knew who I was until I told them my name. One of them ran off to get my brother George whom they said was fishing further downstream.

As George embraced me tears glinted in his eyes.

"It's good to be home," I said. I could feel tears welling up in my own eyes.

"Let me run ahead to call Mum and Dad. They went to bed before we left to go fishing."

He grabbed my suitcase and ran ahead.

I was right behind him and as he called out to our parents to come and see who was home from America. We made so much noise we woke up the neighbours, and they came out to see what the commotion was about.

Dad had a blanket wrapped around him and my mother had a thick bed jacket over her shoulders. They looked as if they had been sound asleep and kept blinking. They couldn't stop hugging me. Nobody said anything for five minutes, we were all crying with joy.

George had made coffees for all of us and he passed them around. Sipping that beautiful thick, black, sweet coffee, and watching the glow of happiness on my parent's faces was the best homecoming I could ever have imagined.

***

George ... not long after coming home from America.

37

This second time he flew he didn't get airsick. So instead of coming back from Sydney on a train as we expected, he went on to Tahiti where he even took a boat trip to Moorea without getting seasick.

We couldn't imagine how anyone convinced him to do that but they did. From Tahiti he flew to Mexico, then to New York where he met some old friends whom he hadn't seen in more than half a century, and finally from there to Greece and via Skopje to Tirana in Albania. Mum of course went with him.

He was met in Tirana by some of his oldest brother's children, now middle aged. They were overjoyed to meet the uncle to whom they had been writing for many years but had never met.

As happy as he was to see someone from his side of the family, he was also apprehensive. Albania was a police state and no one was allowed to wander about unescorted. In fact he was only granted a visa because his nephew worked for the government and could vouch for him.

I've booked you into our best hotel, his nephew told him.

***

He had stared at the cracked facade of the grand old building that masqueraded as a hotel in the heart of Tirana. It looked ready to fall down,

"That's nice," he said with dismay.

"They even have flush toilets in every room," the nephew said with pride.

***

"You should have seen it," the old man said when he came home. "There was a tap and a bucket. When you wanted to flush the toilet you filled the bucket under the tap then tipped the water into the toilet bowl.

38

And they called that modern," he chuckled.

"Better than a hole in the ground that you squat over," we said.

"They've got those too. You've got to be careful you don't step in the hole at night if you have to go."

***

Dervitsani hadn't changed. The houses painted white like those in Argyrokastro sparkled in the clean cold air. The air was so clean I could hardly believe it! Not like in America where the sky in the cities is grey from smoke and the fumes from traffic.

I felt a little dizzy, just breathing that pure air. And I couldn't wait to taste the water. No other country has water like what we have in Greece.

In the morning everyone wanted to talk to me, to welcome me back, to ask what it was like in America, and how did it feel to be home, what my plans were now that I was back.

It was a wonderful morning, but how could I answer them with so many tears in my eyes?

***

I went with my brother George and helped him prepare the small patch he called his farm. I was amazed he had gone back to farming. Compared to the tanning job he had in America this was hard work.

He also operated the flour mill where all the villages took their wheat to be milled into flour. But being towards the end of winter there was not much milling to be done, so he grew vegetables in the family plot until it was time for the wheat to be harvested.

There was snow on the mountains and patches of snow in the deep valleys and the soil was hard because it was still partly frozen.

He wanted to break it up, to turn it over.

"To let it breathe," he said. "This side of the valley is warmer than the other and we can get an earlier crop in if we prepare the soil properly."

***

Christos came down out of the mountains with his sheep to see me when he heard I had come home. He slaughtered one of the animals and we had a feast to celebrate my homecoming. Everyone in the village came and there was much singing and dancing. I was really embarrassed when they insisted I lead the dance. It was a Tsamiko.

The Tsamiko is a warrior's dance, usually only danced by men. It was the favourite dance of the mountain men who fought against the Turks, and the leader is expected to do all kinds of fancy, even acrobatic steps as he leads the other dancers around in a circle.

With George proudly holding the handkerchief I led the dancers around and must have done all right since everyone was clapping me on the back and congratulating me when the dance was over.

"After all those years in America," George said, "you still haven't forgotten how to dance."

***

Things were wild in Albania, with bandits roaming the hills and raiding the Greek villages. Christos had managed to organise some guns which some of the men smuggled in from Greece and we patrolled the village at night to keep the bandits away, but one night he was late coming back with the milk from his sheep, and my parents were worried. It was almost midnight when he showed up as unconcerned as ever, and it was only after a lot of prodding that he finally told us what had happened.

He and his young assistant had just finished milking the sheep when the dog started growling. He looked up to see a number of dark shadows emerge from the rocky landscape. The sun had set some time ago and it was hard to see who these people were but my brother knew they were bandits.

"What have we here?" he said softly to his assistant as he surveyed the number of people surrounding his small flock.

"Shiaku Lapa," the young man said, his voice quivering.

Shiaku Lapa was a bandit who supposedly lived nearby in an Albanian village. He had a reputation for ferocity and was not averse to killing those he didn't like, though no one would admit having ever seen him do that.

The bandits pushed their way through the sheep and confronted my brother.

"I am Shiaku Lapa," the wildest looking man said. He stood nose to nose with my brother and glared at him. "I'm looking for someone named Christos who says he's not afraid of bandits."

"You are looking at him." Christos smiled and spoke in Albanian. "Welcome to my camp. I can offer you fresh milk, or if you prefer I'll get my young helper to slaughter a lamb and we'll roast it."

"Ha! There is no need. We have already done it."

He waved his hand and one of his men came forward holding out a dead lamb.

"That is not one of mine," Christos said.

"How can you tell?"

"Do you know who all of your men are?"

"What kind of question is that?"

"You would know if there is a stranger amongst them."

"In an instant," he snarled.

"Well I know all of my sheep by sight. I would know in an instant if one of them was not mine. That is definitely not one of mine."

41

Taken aback for a moment Shiaku Lapa finally grinned. He knew he had come across a man he could not frighten; a man after his own heart. He liked him, even if he was a Greek. "Prepare the lamb," he snapped towards the man holding it.

"Let us talk," Shiaku Lapa said. He took Christos by the arm and together they strolled amongst the sheep, while his men lit a fire and spitted the tiny lamb on a piece of wood laid across two piles of stones.

"I see you employ one of my people. Is he a good worker?"

"Of course he's good. A very good worker, though he's a bit nervous at the moment."

"Ha, he shouldn't be. We mean neither of you any harm. We are just here for a visit."

While Christos was talking with Shiaku Lapa the sheepdog was quietly moving around the herd, pushing back any strays that were nervous because there were so many men about, nipping at their heels if they seemed skittish, growling softly as it kept the sheep together.

When finally they sat down to share the roasted lamb one of the men pulled out a gun and aimed it at the sheepdog. As he started to pull back the trigger, Christos leaped up and grabbed the man, pulling him around so that he faced him. He also twisted the hand holding the gun so it pointed at the bandit's stomach.

"You will have to shoot me first," he said. His voice hissed through clenched teeth. "And you'd better make sure you kill me outright, because if you don't, you won't live long enough to shoot my dog."

"Put the gun away," Shiaku Lapa snarled.

The man put the gun back inside his jacket and sat down without saying a word, but he glared ferociously at Christos.

"Come, sit and finish your meal," Shiaku Lapa said.

Christos sat down warily, not trusting any of the bandits.

"We came here to be friends. Are there others like you in the village?"

"Of course," Christos said. "They are all like me."

Shiaku Lapa laughed.

When Christos also laughed the bandits relaxed and the meal was quickly finished. Without another word they all got up and disappeared into the darkness, like smoke blown away on the wind, leaving Christos and his helper to bring the milk down into the village unhindered but much later than usual.

***

The old man always loved dancing. Whenever there was a party he would be asked to lead the line. He was light on his feet, and his improvisations were elegant and joyful.

On the anniversary of his fiftieth year in Australia, at 78, he danced a Tsamiko in the kitchen.

"This is in memory of my brother Christos," he told everyone.

We had a big kitchen, and surrounded by family and friends he danced with an athleticism that put most of us younger ones to shame.

Later that night after we'd all had a few drinks, we cornered the old man and teased him about his time in America.

"How were the girls in America?" we asked. "Did you have a girl friend?"

He mumbled something about being too busy working during the day and studying English at night to go out with girls.

"Come on, what about your friends?"

"We were all foreigners, remember. Girls didn't go out with men who couldn't speak English. Things were different then."

"You were all young. Don't tell us you didn't go to one of those places; did they call them brothels then?"

"NO. Never."

"What do you mean never? They didn't call them brothels? Or you never went, not even once?"

He stared at us and blushed.

"I did accompany some of my friends to New York once," he reluctantly admitted, "and we went to one of those places. But I didn't go inside."

"Really?"

"Past the front room, that is, I was too shy. The others went in. I just sat there and waited for them," he eventually said after a bit more teasing.

"You didn't want to go in?"

He shrugged.

"I thought I did. I guess I was too scared, I don't know. I was not used to talking to women, you know. Socially I was very shy."

And that's all he would say.

No amount of teasing or cajoling could elicit another word.

***

After living in America I could not get used to living in the Dervitsani again. It was nothing more than a village. There was nothing to do, no work apart from a little farming or sheep herding and this didn't suit me at all. Besides the farm, George managed a small mill where he ground wheat from the nearby farms into flour. This kept him busy through the late summer and autumn and he seemed quite happy doing this.

The wheat was harvested by hand and tied into bundles.

Each farmer would bring his wheat to the community threshing floor beside the mill where the chaff would be separated from the grain. It was the only concrete floor in the village. It was about fifteen metres across and there was a huge pole in the middle of it. Tall poles around the perimiter held up a crude wooden slatted roof but there were no side walls. The wind had to blow through.

Nothing could pull the central pole over. It had to be strong because to thresh the wheat two horses were used. They were hitched to a rotating ring on the central pole and they walked round and round over the wheat which the farmer scattered across the floor. When the stalks were considered crushed enough, the horses were given a rest. The farmer and his family, and anyone else who wanted to help, would come in and start tossing this crumpled mixture up into the air with large wooden pitchforks. It was usually done when it was windy so the wind could blow the lighter chaff across the floor leaving the heavier grains to be swept up and bagged.

The bags of wheat were then taken to the mill so George could grind it into flour. Sometimes George would be paid in cash for his service, but more often than not his only payment was a percentage of the flour produced. He often gave some of this to the baker who in turn gave us fresh loaves of bread to take home; and the baker also didn't charge us anything when Mum wanted to bake a lamb in his oven because ours wasn't big enough.

During the winter when you couldn't cook on a spit in the open the women often took their lamb and stuffed capsicums to the baker to have it cooked in his oven. He never charged much but he made more money doing this than selling the bread he made because a lot of families made their own bread. The smell of roasted lamb mingled with the yeasty aroma of freshly baked bread was irresistible.

It was not an uncommon sight in the early evening to see lots of women hurrying down the streets with trays of roasted meat steaming in the frosty air as they rushed to get home before the dinner got cold.

I helped George for a time, but after a few months I realised there was no future for me in Dervitsani.

America had changed me, and I wanted to go back.

***

This was about the time the bandits took that young boy from our village and held him for ransom.

I remember seeing the boy's mother running down the main street screaming with all the power her lungs could put out: "They've taken my son, they've taken my son," she kept repeating.

She waved the ransom note in the air.

"They want two hundred sovereigns. Where am I going to find two hundred sovereigns?"

She stopped in front of a Kafeneion where many of the single men were drinking coffee and Arak, or playing backgammon.

"Which one of you brave men will go up into the mountains to bring back my son?"

None of them would look at her.

"Cowards," she screeched, "worthless good for nothings."

Of course everyone knew her son. He was a wild lad of about sixteen years. He was outspoken, and often critical of the Albanians, some of whom had obviously taken offence to this and had decided to teach him and the other Greeks a lesson. They were threatening to kill him if the ransom wasn't paid.

That night the town council held a meeting. There was no problem raising the money, everyone put in what they could and soon enough the council had the amount asked for. The problem was: who would take the money to the bandits and bring back the boy?

When this question came up everyone seemed to have important things to do, even those whose habit it was to while away the days drinking coffee or Arak in the Kafeneions.

The place where the bandits wanted them to hand over the money in exchange for the boy was in the mountains, a remote pass far from any village, and the time set was midnight. No one wanted to go, since none of them trusted the bandits. They were frightened they would be killed and the money stolen. They were all convinced they would never see the boy again.

They asked me if I would ask my brother Christos to help.

He knew the mountains well. He also knew Shiaku Lapa, and

they thought this would help. Everyone knew of Christos' encounter with Shiaku Lapa and how they had eaten a roasted lamb together.

I found Christos at home. He had just come down with the sheep's milk so Mum could make butter, and when I told him what had happened he was furious. Especially when I said no one was willing to risk themselves by going after the boy.

"It's not Shiaku Lapa", Christos said as we walked back to the place where the meeting was. "He wouldn't stoop so low. Steal a sheep, or a bag of wheat, maybe kill someone he didn't like; but to kidnap kids and hold them for ransom... No, That's not him. It's not his style."

Back at the meeting Christos berated the others for their cowardice. "Give me the money," he said finally. "I'll go and get the boy."

"I think I know who is behind this," Christos said as we made our way back home. "Do you remember the one I told you about who wanted to kill my dog? I'll bet it's him. He split up with Shiaku Lapa some time ago."

"What if it's not him? What if it's no one you know? They might just do what everyone is frightened of, kill you and the boy and keep the money anyway. Why should you trust them?"

"You can only die once," Christos said, "and if that's the way it's going to happen, I'll just have to accept it".

He looked atme then laughed at the worried expression on my face. "Hey little brother you worry too much. I'll pretend Shiaku Lapa is a good friend of mine. They all know him. He's king of the bandits around here. Everyone respects him."

"He's not really your friend is he?"

"No. But only we know that."

He laughed and slapped me on the shoulders hard enough to make me stagger forwards.

"Don't look so downhearted," he said as he went to prepare for his meeting in the mountains. "I'll bring back the lad, and with a bit of luck I'll bring back the money too."

"I'll come with you. I can watch your back. Get me a gun."

"No. No guns. We go unarmed to show them that we are genuine; that we hold no malice towards them. They do what they have to do in order to survive just as we also do what we have to."

So Christos and I went up into the mountains that night.

We had sheepskin cloaks thrown over our shoulders and caps pulled down over our ears because it was a cold night even though it was the middle of summer. We looked very much like bandits ourselves.

It was a clear night and the dampness settling out of the air made the rocks glisten in the moonlight. We had barely walked into the rendezvous area when we were challenged and ordered to stop.

Two men, both with rifles pointed at us, with belts of bullets slung across their shoulders came out from behind large boulders.

"Are you armed?" one of then snarled.

"No," Christos said. "I'm only carrying money. Isn't that what you asked for?"

The one who had spoken stepped forward while the other kept his rifle pointed at Christos and me. He checked to see if Christos was telling the truth about not being armed, but when he tried to take the bag of money from Christos pocket he found his hand suddenly grasped in a powerful grip which forced him to let go.

"I'll carry that," Christos told him quietly.

"As you wish," the bandit said. He turned abruptly and started walking towards the huge boulders scattered along the roadside. We followed and as the other bandit fell in behind me I felt a strange sensation in the middle of my back. There was no doubt in my mind he had his rifle pointed right at me and any suspicious move on my part would result in a bullet in the back.

It was only a short walk along a narrow path to a small cave. A fire spluttered half heartedly inside the entrance.

The damp mountain air prevented the smoke from escaping and

the cave was dirty and gloomy. The smoke made Christos' eyes water as he sat cross legged facing several men whose faces he couldn't see. I sat further back, not a part of the negotiations. The men wore black hoods pulled forward so their faces were in shadow. There was an occasional glint in the shadowed faces as light from the flickering fire reflected off their eyes.

"Where is the boy?" Christos asked.

"He's in another cave," the bandit in the middle answered.

"Did you bring the money?" One of the others asked.

"Yes," Christos said. "But I think you ask too much. The boy is useless. He does nothing but drink coffee and laze about all day, then expects his poor mother to feed him."

"We ask only two hundred sovereigns."

"Much too much," Christos said. He pulled out a tobacco pouch and papers, calmly rolled a cigarette. "Do you want one?"

He offered the cigarette to the man in the middle.

No one moved for a few moments then the man in the middle asked: "How much do you think the boy is worth?"

They were all taken aback by Christos' audacity. They had expected he would be nervous or frightened, yet here he was, as calm as you like, telling them they were asking too much. I was the one who was nervous so it was a good thing no one decided to speak to me.

"They are poor people in my village," Christos said. "If you want sheep, you can have sheep. Take some of mine. You want wheat, barley, water melons? They have all of those things. It is money they do not have."

"But it is money we want," the bandit stated.

"You want too much," Christos told them again. He put the cigarette in his mouth and struck a match as if to light it. But instead, he held the match out in front of him so he could see the faces of the bandits. "So it's you," he said scornfully. "I thought I recognised your voice."

The face the lighted match revealed was that of the man who

had tried to shoot his dog, the night he had first encountered Shiaku Lapa.

"Take me to Shiaku Lapa," Christos said. "I'll deal with him."

There was a moment's hesitation followed by: "We're not with him anymore. We didn't see eye to eye so some of us have gone out on our own."

"So he kicked you out."

There was absolute silence. The only noise in the cave was the feeble spluttering of the fire. Now you've done it, I thought.

Christos also realised he had gone too far. So before they could decide to shoot him, he chuckled and said that Shiaku Lapa, if ever he had decided to kidnap this boy he would never have asked for more than fifty sovereigns, because he would have known that's all our village could raise.

Before leaving for this rendezvous Christos had divided the money into four equal lots placing them in various locations on his person. He took out one bag of money and held it towards the man in the middle.

"Fifty sovereigns. Here it is." He shook the bag so the money it contained made some noise. "Now why don't you send someone to get the boy?"

The man in the middle leaned forward never once taking his brittle eyes off Christos face. He took the bag of money and tipped it onto the ground in front of him so he could see it was actual money.

"Get the boy," he said, and someone behind me moved. I could hear him scrambling down the rocky slope outside the cave.

Finally the bandit looked down. He picked the money up piece by piece, checking to see if there really were fifty sovereigns there.

When he had put all the money back into the bag he looked at Christos and said: "Go back to your village. The boy is waiting outside."

It was almost three AM when Christos, myself and the boy came down out of the mountains.

Everyone had been anxiously waiting and when they knew the result, there was a great celebration. Christos gave the remaining money to the Town Council members and all of them insisted on having a glass of Ouzo with him.

When they started to get rowdy, he slipped away for a couple of hours of sleep.

He was gone in the morning when the sun came up, back into the mountains to look after his sheep.

***

I wrote to the American consulate in Tirana and was told I could apply for re-migration but I would have to go on a waiting list.

Immigration to America had been closed and each country had been given a quota. The number allowed to emigrate from Albania was small and there were many more people wanting to go than would be allowed in. I was urged to apply as soon as possible and this I did, travelling all the way to the consulate in Tirana and handing in my application in person.

I was given a number and the man who allocated the number to my file looked at me with a blank expression on his face and said: "Three years."

"Three years for what?" I asked.

"You will probably have to wait three years, maybe more."

"That's ridiculous…"

"Do you want to be on the waiting list?"

Well of course I did. I didn't come all this way for nothing.

The man was still looking at me, his face devoid of any expression of compassion. He didn't care what I did.

"Yes," I finally said. "Put me on the list."

The man nodded, scribbled something on my file, and looked straight at me.

"We'll let you know when your number comes up," and with that he turned away, closed my file and pushed it to the side of his desk where other papers were stacked haphazardly. He was done with me.

***

With the flour mill and our small farm, our family was reasonably prosperous compared to some of the others in the village. Christos' sheep supplied the milk to make fetta cheese, of which there was enough to sell in one of the local shops. My father was a school teacher, and my mother used to do a bit of extra sewing at home. Naturally I helped her with that also, since I was a qualified tailor, but there was no real work for a tailor in our village.

The people in general were too poor to buy suits made by someone else. Apart from their Sunday best, which was something that lasted them a lifetime, all their other clothes were home made.

Mum and Dad.

Mum's picture was taken sometime in the 1930s Dad's picture was taken long before that.

***

Winter came, then Spring with wild flowers bursting out all over the slopes around the valley. The air was filled with a beautiful scent and buzzed with bees gathering honey.

I had heard nothing from the American consul and was becoming increasingly impatient. My parents wanted me to get married, but this was the last thing on my mind. There were lots of pretty girls but the only thing on my mind was going back to America.

I decided I would once again go to Tirana and find out what the delay was.

I had no trouble getting in to see the Consul, and he assured me that my application had been accepted. He even showed me a document with my number on it.

"You must wait," he said.

"How long?" I wanted to know.

"Anything up to three years."

"But that's what you told me more than a year ago."

He shrugged just like he did that other time. And like that other time his face again became devoid of expression as if he was bored with my enquiry. There were probably thousands of people like me who continued to pester him about how long they had to wait. He couldn't have cared less.

"That is all I can tell you at the moment. You will be notified when your turn comes."

And with that I was again dismissed.

What could I do? I went home to wait.

***

The question of marriage came up again. My sister was long married and happily living in her husband's village several kilometres away in another valley. According to my parents, I was getting too old not to be married.

"Look at your brothers," they said. "Both of them are married and are already fathers."

And fine children they had too, I acknowledged silently, but was that what I wanted? I didn't know. They were both older than me. It was only right that they should be married before me.

All my thoughts were filled with the overwhelming idea of going back to America. As far as I was concerned that was where the future was.

***

I waited, and waited, growing more impatient as each day went by and still no notice came from the American Consul.

Once again my parents brought up the subject of marriage.

They even suggested a number of fine young ladies, so reluctantly I agreed to get married, more to please them rather than myself.

Once having made the decision however, I was quite happy. It was a relief, really. You don't realise how much pressure people put on you to conform until that pressure is gone, and in our village it was no different.

People spoke to me in a more friendly way. I hadn't realised until that moment that they had treated me differently. I was the one who had gone away and returned, but who wanted to go away again. With them knowing that, they treated me in a friendly way, but with some reserve. They acted, I could see now, as if they wanted to ostracise me for bringing into the village a discontentment with the way things were; but they were unable to do so because I was one of them. I had been born in this village. My parents lived here and were well known. My brothers lived here, cousins, uncles. I was as much a part of this village as the rest of them. But they saw me as a disturbing influence on the other young men who all wanted to hear what it was like in America, and who if they could, would do what I had done.

They had probably treated my parents differently also, and this was perhaps the reason they were so anxious for me to get married. So I kept quiet about wanting to go to America again.

I did what was asked of me, worked hard at whatever jobs came up, though I wasn't suited to farm work, and settled into married life.

***

"Our weddings were different from what you have here in Australia," the old man said over a cup of hot black coffee one Sunday. He would often reminisce about life in the village where he was born when we were sitting and drinking coffee.

"First of all," he said, "boys and girls were not allowed to go out with each other. If a boy liked a certain girl and wanted to marry her he would have to tell his mother. She would then get in touch with the girl's parents indirectly and propose a meeting in which one of the boy's male relatives, usually an uncle would make an official proposal on the boy's behalf."

"Sounds pretty complicated."

"Ah, but that's the way it was done."

"What if the girl didn't like the boy?"

"Nothing would happen. You have to realise that everyone in the village knew everyone else, and if the girl did like the boy, then the engagement would become official. A date would be agreed upon by both families for the wedding. There was no dowry, but the prospective groom was expected to pay a sum of money to the bride which she would give to her parents. They would use this to buy such things as a mattress and some blankets, pillows and a bedspread, and a small trunk full of underwear for the bride. All this stuff was loaded on a horse and delivered on the same day as the wedding procession.

In fact it was part of the procession. So whatever the groom paid he got back in this way.

"Once the date was set, usually a few months away, invitations are sent out to all the relatives and friends on both sides. This often means the whole village. Preparations are made, you know, how many sheep have to be slaughtered, who will make the bread, the salads, and so on. Everyone has to help.

"The wedding always takes place on a Sunday, but the festivities start on Saturday and don't finish until Monday, and sometimes even Tuesday.

"On the day of the wedding the guests begin to arrive at the groom's house early in the morning. Most people bring something to eat; a leg of lamb, a skin or a bottle of wine, cheese and bread. They'll have some lunch there while the groom dresses in his new clothes. When the band arrives, usually a group with a clarinet, a violin, a banjo or bouzouki, and a large tambour, the real fun begins.

"The band of musicians will lead the way. They will be followed of course by the groom and his parents and guests, singing and dancing as they go along the streets leading to the bride's house where her family's guests are waiting. Toasts are made, savouries are eaten and wine is drunk while they mingle and wait until the bride is ready.

"As soon as the bride is ready a white horse is brought out for her to ride on. If they don't have a white horse they'll cover one with flour so it looks white. A young maiden will lead the horse while the bride, her face hidden with a long veil sits quietly on the horse as if apart from the festivities going on around her. She will pretend to be aloof, but you can bet she'll be watching everything that's happening.

"The ceremony takes about an hour in the church after which the bride whose face is still covered with a veil remounts the horse. This time one of the groom's younger relatives will lead the horse to the husband's place. Of course the musicians will be playing, and people will be singing and dancing in the streets as they go along.

"Before the bride can dismount however a guest will offer her some money to do so. No specific amount, just whatever he can afford... And it's the same with the unveiling. A relative of the husband will offer the bride some gold or silver coins to remove the veil. While this is going on the musicians will play a bridal song and the women will all sing a special song wishing her a long and happy life.

"At the end of the night as people start to leave the bride and her hand maidens will line up by the door, and holding the coins they have received they will jingle them in their left hands while thanking the guests for coming and for the gifts they have brought. Each male guest on departing will receive a kiss from the bride while he puts into her right hand a coin or coins, whatever he feels he can afford, as a further gift, and in this way the bride receives a lot of money to give her and her husband a good start in life."

For a long time the old man sat and started at the grains of coffee in the bottom of his cup, not saying anything.

Then he looked up. "It doesn't happen like that anymore," he said. "Hasn't for a long time... Ever since the communists took over and banned religion and Atheism became official. A wedding there now is nothing more than walking into an office and signing a register. All you need is an official witness and it's done."

***

Most of the younger men sat in the kafeneion drinking endless cups of coffee, talking, and playing backgammon with frightening ferocity. They would slam the tokens down, glaring and sometimes yelling at each other, though never coming to blows. It was the frustration and boredom of having nothing to do showing through.

There was not much work apart from seasonal farm work, so there was a lot of dissatisfaction. Many wanted to leave but were afraid, unable to imagine what it could be like in a big city, or anywhere else outside their village, and those that could go, and who like me wanted to go to America were on an endlessly long waiting list.

A few had just recently left for Australia having given up waiting to go to America.

The others kept asking me what it was like in America, and the more I talked about it the more I wanted to leave, to go back.

I didn't want to be a farmer, to work in the fields all my life. I didn't want to be sheep herder, or a miller. I wanted to work at my own trade. I was good at it and I knew I could make a comfortable living. I had been to Tirana and no matter what people here thought of it, as a city it simply didn't compare to anything in America.

And to work as a tailor, I needed to be in a city where there was the possibility of many customers who needed to wear suits daily rather than once a week on Sunday, or occasionally at a wedding or a funeral.

When my daughter was born I had ambivalent feelings.

As happy as I was to see that tiny little face for the first time, the thoughts that kept dominating were about what future she would have in a small village like ours. I looked around and saw nothing but drudgery and hard work. With little education available the future for a woman in a village like ours would only be bleak. There would be none of the freedom that women in America enjoyed.

I knew little of the rest of the world and could only compare our village life with that of the cities in America where I had been, and the comparison was not good. Even Tirana where I had gone to make my application at the American Consulate was nothing more than a bloated village.

The birth of my daughter was what finally made up my mind.

If I couldn't go to America I would go to Australia or Argentina. Both of these countries actively encouraged immigration, so we heard.

America had closed its doors, we were told over and over again, and it looked very likely that neither my number nor anyone else's would ever come up.

***

They spoke English in Australia.

I couldn't speak Spanish so Argentina was out; but my English was very good after seven years in America, so Australia it would have to be.

I had waited almost three years for the chance to return to America but finally my patience ran out. It was a hard decision to make, knowing that this time I would not come back. But this time I would have my own family with me and that would make a big difference. I would not be alone.

I sat down with my older brother George and discussed ways and means of raising enough money for the fare to Australia.

It was a lot more expensive than going to America.

There was no way I could travel with my wife and daughter; we just couldn't raise enough money. But we could manage it if I went alone. Once I got to Australia I could get a job and save money. If the pay was anywhere as good as in America it wouldn't be long before I would have enough to bring out my wife and daughter.

I didn't want to leave without them, but there was no other way to do it.

Word soon got around that I was thinking of going to Australia. Quite a few other young men wanted to go as well, so they came to see me to ask about how they could do it. They were all excited about the prospect. For weeks that's all anyone in the village talked about: Going to Australia.

From the Australian Consul in Greece we found out what we needed to know and eventually we numbered seven, those who had decided for certain to make the trip. All of us went to Argyrokas-tro where we arranged to get Albanian Passports, since officially we were living in Albania and the government considered us to be citizens regardless of what we ourselves thought.

We didn't leave though, until the end of October. We had to help with the harvesting.

***

This time I left with the others on the back of a truck.

We had thrown our bags up and there was nothing left to do but to say goodbye. The whole village was there to see us off.

No sneaking off in the middle of the night this time. We were free to go. The Turks had been kicked out of Albania and although we were Greeks we were travelling as free Albanians.

Saying goodbye this time was different.

It was much sadder because everyone knew we would not be coming back.

I was not aware of my father or my two older brothers, or even of my wife, all of whom were there.

I was only aware of my mother who was holding my daughter in one arm. She was crying and she hugged me to her with her free arm. I tried to tell her that I would see her again, but even if I believed it at that moment, she knew it was a lie. She hung on tight and cried. I couldn't help it either. Tears poured out of my eyes.

Finally my mother pushed me away. A tiny smile quivered at the edge of her lips and she said: "You'd better go. The others are waiting for you."

I kissed her one final time. I gave my daughter a peck on the cheek. She was only ten months old and had no idea of what was going on.

The others were calling to me to hurry up because the driver wanted to go. I climbed up onto the back of the truck, then the driver cranked the engine and it spluttered into life. There was a crunch as he shoved it into gear and the truck lurched forward. Everyone waved, and we waved back.

I was still waving as the truck went over a rise and down the other side.

I finally stopped waving when the village disappeared, but I kept staring back towards it for a long time.

I could not imagine then that it would be more than fifty years before I would ever see it again, and that everyone I had known would all have died.

***

"Hey, are you still crying?" One of the men in the truckasked.

All of them were excited and couldn't understand why I was sad.

I couldn't explain it to them, or to myself.

It was such a beautiful sunny day with the mountain air so crisp and clean it made me feel as if I had drunk a little too much wine, and my compatriots' enthusiasm for the journey ahead was so contagious, that my sadness at leaving my family behind was pushed aside.

We sang songs as the truck laboured over the rough roads leading down to the border with Greece.

***

In 1975, standing near the Acropolis and looking out across one of Europe's most polluted and dirty cities, the old man remembered how clear the air was in 1924 when he and the others had arrived here for the first time. How the marble of the Acropolis sparkled in the sunshine.

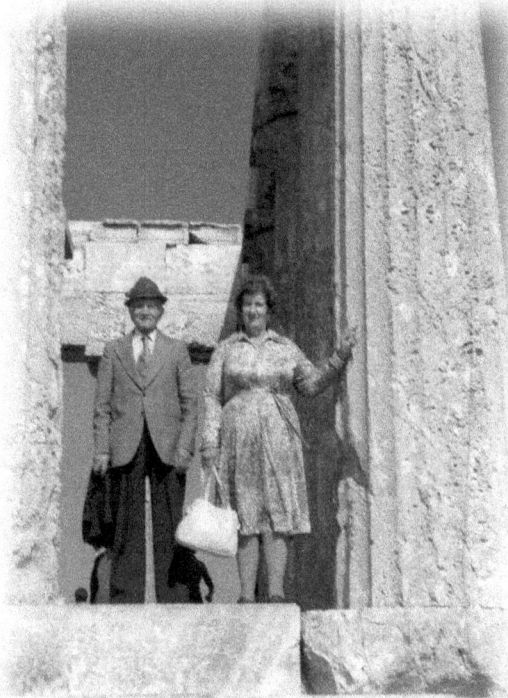

Athens was not so big then. There was no acid rain eating into the marble of the ancient statues and buildings, no photochemical smog eating holes in people's lungs. It was a beautiful clean city with clear air, and everywhere you looked you could see things with a sharpness and clarity that was generated by the peculiar light from the sun of Greece.

No other country he had been in glowed the way Greece did then.

Now it is like the rest of the world, he thought, smudged and faded. Or is it just that my old eyes don't see as well as they once did?

***

Athens seen from the Acropolis around 1975

We stayed a month in Athens, while waiting for an Italian ship called Red Italia. It was a well used ship by the look of it but not a lot bigger than the one I had travelled to America on. I was hoping that it wouldn't move around too much and perhaps I wouldn't get as sea-sick as I had those times before. I wasn't really looking forward to travelling by ship, but there was no other way to get to Australia.

Quite by accident we found an Epirotic cafe where we met a lot of people from our own part of Greece so none of us felt very homesick. There was a lot of singing and dancing, a lot of gossiping and we all had a great time. It was just like being on a holiday.

The only thing that marred our stay was the long wait we had at the immigration department where we went to get our clearances for Australia. We were made to wait for hours while others who had come in after us went ahead.

All they had to do was stamp our passport and sign the visa. What was the delay? Why was it taking so long?

The man at the counter processing the passports kept glancing our way as often as he kept pushing our documents aside to process others who had come in after us. He kept glancing our way but when ever I caught him at it he would look away and shuffle the passports stacked up on his desk.

Finally I figured out what the delay was. It was our passports. They were Albanian, not Greek. He kept pushing them aside. He and the other staff were treating us as if we were foreigners. They thought we were Albanians and Greeks didn't like Albanians.

But we were as Greek as the rest of them.

Was it our fault that we happened to have been born and lived in a part of Greece that was no longer Greek territory but was land stolen from our country?

Was it our fault that we were given Albanian passports when we got permission to leave?

I was furious. No more waiting... I'd had enough of waiting.

I went over and demanded to see the man in charge.

When I finally got in to see this man in his more private office I reminded him after asking what the delay was, that we also were Greeks and that we had been dispossessed of our nationality by the Great Powers who decreed where the borders of each country were established. I told him in no uncertain terms that our ancestors had fought with his against the Turks, and that we should be treated as equals.

Didn't we also speak the Greek language?

Did he not remember that Epirus was the birthplace of the Greek language?

Besides it would only take a few seconds to stamp and sign our passports.

He stared at me for a few minutes, obviously taken aback that someone would have the audacity to question his authority.

Perhaps he didn't expect someone who was leaving the country to be so forceful. Did he expect us to act like sheep?

Finally he smiled and apologised. "No matter the passport," he said, "you are obviously Greek and should have gone in turn, like everyone else. Bring the others in; I'll fix them all right now. My staff shouldn't do things like that."

It was all bullswool, but at least we got our passports stamped and signed.

Finally the day came when we could board the Red Italia.

It was the end of October 1924. By Christmas we would be in Australia.

***

This time the weather was much better, and the sea was nowhere near as turbulent as it had been when I crossed the Atlantic to America. But the waves were bigger... huge waves, like mountains. How I hated the way the ship shuddered as it climbed the sides of those huge waves.

It is impossible to imagine how much water there is in the Oceans. It goes on for ever.

This time I knew what to expect. Of course I got sea sick, but I could alleviate it by sitting up on deck. I even slept there.

Right up on the top deck where the air was always fresh. The main thing was to get away from the smell of vomit down in the third class areas of the ship where our cabins were located. It didn't stop me from being sick, but it made it bearable. I could actually eat a little and keep it down, which was a good thing since the trip to Australia was a lot longer than the trip to America.

How we all envied the two youngsters in our group who never got seasick. And both of them only seventeen years old! They were like sailors. They never felt the movement of the ship.

They helped clean up the mess we made, they brought food and water to those who could not make it to the dining room, and they were constantly cheerful. They tried very hard to keep our spirits up, which was difficult since there is no person more depressed than one who suffers from severe sea sickness. As long as the ship moves, there is no escape. As long as there is no escape you would rather be dead than alive.

***

On December the 24th, 1924 Albania was declared a Republic. Ahmed Zogou was no longer the Prime Minister. But he would come back a year later to take over the country once again. In 1928 he would declare himself King changing his name to Zog.

***

December the 24th 1924 was the day we arrived in Adelaide.

Everyone was excited because at long last we had arrived and could get off the ship. We weren't allowed off in Fremantle where quite a few passengers disembarked.

At sea again, after leaving Perth's port of Fremantle, sailing along the coast from time to time we caught glimpses of distant jagged cliffs that seemed to stretch endlessly into the haze ahead of us. We were never close enough to see any details.

"There's nothing to see," one of the sailors told us. "That's the Great Australian Bight. There's nothing there for miles, just the Nullabor. It's flat and empty right to the cliff edge."

After that explanation he wandered off to coil a long rope that had been spread along the deck while we all stared at the distant edge of Australia. I tried to imagine what it might be like but I knew nothing at all about Australia and so my mind remained blank. But it did feel good to have finally arrived.

In Adelaide we were allowed off the ship for three hours.

It was absolutely wonderful to walk on dry land, to stand on something that wasn't moving, to look around and see buildings and streets, houses and cars, instead of endless heaving mountains of water.

A small group of us wandered along a narrow street not far from the docks. There was a small shop near the end of the street and we decided it would be nice to have a drink, so we went in.

To our utter astonishment there was standing behind the counter of this shop a man from our own village.

I could not believe it. He had left our village only a couple of months before we did, but had never told anyone where he was going. He had never mentioned Australia. Everyone thought he had gone to Argyrokastro. And here he was in Australia!

And working in the very shop we happened to walk into.

"What are you doing here?" was all anyone could think of asking.

He just laughed. "Why, the same thing you are, of course."

We were all excited and tried to convince him to come to Melbourne with us, but he declined.

"I've just started working here," he told us. "It's good to be working and earning some money. I just can't leave like that."

He wouldn't let us pay for our drinks, telling us that we would need every penny we had for when we arrived in Melbourne.

We didn't know what he meant but it was nice of him to offer us the drinks.

We were not to know as we wandered happily back to the ship for the last leg of our journey to Melbourne, that most of us would never see our compatriot in the milk bar again, that he would disappear into the vastness of Australia, and that through a simple mistake and a lack of ability to speak English, he would be lost to us for twenty years.

***

Once the ship was again at sea, the captain made an announcement that dismayed all of us.

He stated unequivocally: "The Australian immigration department requires every migrant coming to Australia to have 10 Pounds ($20), or the equivalent which could be exchanged for Australian money, before they would be allowed to land."

We were told bluntly that any immigrant who did not have the 10 Pounds would not be allowed ashore. That person would remain on the ship and be returned when the ship went back to Greece.

This was dreadful news. I couldn't believe it. We were not told of this requirement before leaving Greece. The official who had stamped our passports and signed the visas never said a word about it. I wonder if that was deliberate because of the way I had confronted him.

None of us had as much money as they wanted. I looked around and saw that a few people I knew who could also speak English seemed quite upset.

"I'm sorry." The Captain's voice had softened. "But those are the regulations."

When I told my compatriots what the Captain had said they were all stunned.

"But we can't go back," one of them said.

"To come all this way for nothing," another muttered, then he looked at me and said, "I'll jump over the side and swim ashore."

"Can you swim?" I asked.

"It doesn't matter. One way or another I'm getting off this ship."

"Let's just calm down and think about it," I said. "Tomorrow is Christmas day and we won't arrive in Melbourne until the day after. We'll think of something by then."

Christmas dinner was a gloomy affair with no one in much of a mood for celebrating. The Captain didn't appear; no doubt to avoid questions or entreaties people might throw at him. We sat around feeling depressed. Some other groups seemed to be enjoying themselves so they must have been all right as far as the money was concerned. Either that, or they simply did not understand the situation that would apply upon arrival in Melbourne.

The ship heaved and rolled along making all of us feel sicker than ever. What could we do? None of us wanted to go back.

I couldn't sleep that night, and in the morning as the ship

Re d'Italia, arriving in Melbourne on Boxing Day 1924.

lurched through the entrance to Port Phillip Bay I had a desperate idea.

"How much money have you got?" I asked one of my friends.

"I don't know, perhaps a bit over a pound."

"What about you?"

"The same I suppose."

"Me too," another said.

"And I would have about two pounds," I said. "What if put all our money together and took it to the purser to exchange for Australian money, would we have enough?"

"There'd probably be enough for one, but what about the rest of us? We each need ten pounds, remember. That's a lot of money."

"Okay. This is what we'll do," I told them. "We get the money changed and see how much it is. There are a lot Greeks on board who can't speak English so when the immigration officials come on board to interview each passenger I'll ask them if I can assist them as an interpreter. I'm sure they'll accept the offer. I'll pretend the money is mine and show it to them. They'll see I have more than enough. Then I'll pass it back to you. Each one of you will do the same. You will use the same money. Show it to them and be on your way. Then pass it back to the next one. Just don't stay too close to each other in the queue or they'll get suspicious."

"That's a stupid idea."

"Have you got a better one?"

They were all silent. I could see them weighing the idea, considering its possibilities. Then one by one they nodded.

"Let's do it," everyone agreed.

Each of us raced back to our bunks and packed our belongings. The money was pooled and exchanged. It came to almost fifteen pounds. Back on the main deck we watched with interest as the ship was eased up to the side of the pier by a couple of tugboats. The gangplank went down and the immigration officials came aboard.

Once they had settled themselves at a long trestle across the main deck I went up and asked them if they wanted an interpreter.

I was nervous, and worried they might say no.

They conferred for a few moments, then one of them said: "That would be a big help. What's your name?"

"Spiro Litchen" I told them and they looked it up in their files.

"Not on this list," the man said after a long time spent looking at the rows of names.

Of course not, that was my name in America. We were using Albanian passports so my name should be in Albanian not English or Greek."Try Spiro Lici," I suggested.

"Say that again."

"I'll write it down for you." I took a pen he held out and wrote it phonetically in English on a pad he had in front of him.

"Okay," he said with a smile having found it on the list. Page 28 passenger number 602 travelling 3rd class.

"Do you have ten pounds?"

"I've got more than that. There's almost fifteen pounds here." I showed it to them.

"That's good. We'll be starting in a few minutes, take a seat."

"I'll just go back and tell my friends that I'll be up here with you."

"Righto mate."

I took that to mean yes.

I raced back to my friends. "It's working," I told them. I handed the money to one of them. "Now spread out and do it the way we planned and we should all get through."

As each one of my compatriots came up to the table, and answered the questions asked, he showed the 15 Pounds to the official who noted it on a form. His papers were stamped and handed over, then he was free to go ashore. While strolling casually back along the queue to collect his baggage, he would quickly pass the money to the next one in our group who would then follow the same procedure.

There was a lot of confusion and people milling about since

there were several queues being processed simultaneously so I was sure our passing of the money from one to another would not have been noticed, at least not by the others waiting in the queues.

I wondered if anyone else was doing the same as us.

I had a suspicion that the officials I was interpreting for knew what was going on, but they never said anything. As long as the prospective immigrant standing in front of them showed he had the required amount of money with him at that moment they allowed him to land. Where the money came from was not their concern.

This was a good country. I was convinced of that already, and I hadn't even got off the ship yet. I was glad I had made the decision to come here.

Once everyone had been processed, the officials all shook hands with me and wished me luck. They thanked me and at last I was free to join my compatriots ashore.

I ran down the gangplank thinking that if to leave this country meant travelling by ship, I would not do it.

I was here to stay and would make the most of it no matter what happened.

I joined my friends on the pier, thinking how wonderful it felt to be walking on solid land. It was a beautiful day. The sun shone on a sparkling sea, and in the distance the city of Melbourne beckoned.

***

"The Station hasn't changed a bit," the old man said one day when we were in town together. "The only difference is the clocks are all electronic now. They used to have someone come out every few minutes with a long metal pole to reach up and change the times on the clocks as well as the signs with the train destinations on them.

There was always someone poking and shoving at those signs and clocks."

"It's all been rebuilt inside," I told him.

"That's nothing. There are still the same numbers of platforms, and the outside hasn't changed. It looks as scruffy as ever. It's the outside I remember, with all the shallow steps, and the clocks."

He marched up the steps and stood under the clocks.

"This is where we stood when we first walked out of the station."

He looked around, his eyes seeing beyond the traffic in Flinders Street, back to the time he and his friends stood there feeling lost, not knowing where to go.

"We were dressed in our best clothes, and we had our suitcases and bags with us. Everyone could see we were strangers, but no one offered to help us. There were people everywhere, crossing the street, hurrying up the steps to go into the station to catch their trains. Others pushed past us as they came out of the station. Everyone ignored us. It's like we were invisible." He paused and then said, "There were others like us too, standing under the clocks."

"They could've been waiting for someone," I suggested, but he didn't hear me.

"No one thought to ask us if we were lost."

***

There was a long train waiting on the pier and a lot of people getting off the ship went straight onto the train. It was an old train with dark red carriages and wooden seats. It looked like something from the previous century, but it was electric so it could not have been that old. Since I was the only one who could talk English, I was nominated to ask the man in the navy blue uniform standing by the end of the train if it was going into the city.

"It's go-ina Flinders Street," he mumbled.

I couldn't understand him.

"Is that in the city?" I asked carefully.

"A course it's in the bloody city," he snapped.

"Well?" One of my friends asked me.

"I think he said yes."

So we all got on the train. We didn't have to buy any tickets. At least no one came on board to tell us we should, so we settled down to wait for the train to leave. I wasn't game to ask the man about tickets. I could hardly understand anything he said in any case. So we waited, and the train left after a while.

It didn't stop until it got to Flinders street station.

Everyone got off so we did too. On the ship's passenger lists we had been given an address in Melbourne because we had to put something down for the Immigration Authorities. It was 1237 Melbourne Street, Melbourne. I didn't think such a place actually existed. It was a fictitious address. We were told later that there was a Melbourne Road in Williamstown.

But there we were, finally in the heart of Melbourne, and with absolutely no idea where to go We stood under the clocks in front of the station for what seemed a long time and not one person took any notice of us.

***

Regardless of the odd reception I liked Melbourne right from the first day.

It wasn't that big, but it was a city you could move around in. It was like an American city with its long straight streets dividing it into blocks, so you could find your way around without too much trouble.

And it was full of trees, and parks and gardens.

It had a wonderful sense of openness, a city full of fresh air.

European cities are cramped and clustered, old and claustrophobic, decrepit and dying. Here there was a sense of life. I could feel the energy in the air. It seemed to me it was a city that was growing, and I wanted to be a part of that.

I also liked the fact that the streets had names, not numbers like they do in America. Names give places an identity.

They make it more human.

***

On the ship we had met a couple of men from Crete who were returning to Australia after a trip to Greece. They told us that there were a number of Greek clubs in the city but the best one was The Acropolis club in Lonsdale Street.

I went over to one of the men changing the time on the clocks.

"Excuse me, can you direct us to Lonsdale Street."

"That way," he said, pointing vaguely towards Swanston Street. "It's about four blocks."

I wasn't quite sure about the direction, but before I could ask anything else he walked around me.

"Do you mind? I have to change the clocks."

He fiddled about with his long metal pole, altering the time on the clock directly above my head.

"That way," he said again, and pointed directly towards Swanston Street.

***

In Swanston Street we found a restaurant called Hellas.

The Greek man behind the counter came out onto the footpath

when we asked him about The Acropolis club and explained to us how to get there.

Two-carriage trams rattled along the street, with sparks flying from the electric wires where one line crossed another at street corners. The second small carriage was open and people sat contentedly on long benches soaking up the sunshine. More people filled the footpaths, some eating as they walked along.

We found Lonsdale Street and turned in the direction the man from Hellas Cafe, had indicated.

And immediately we felt at home. Here were shops with Greek writing on the windows. There was a Kafeneion with a couple of tables outside, and people drinking our kind of coffee, and a shop with books and newspapers all printed in Greek. The sound of bouzouki wafted from the door., Greek voices, speaking words we could understand. I couldn't help smiling at the irony of it. We could very well have been walking down a street in Athens, even the hot dusty weather felt the same, yet here we were on the other side of the world at the end of our long journey, in Australia, in Melbourne.

***

"Welcome, welcome," the proprietor said as we dropped our bags at the top of the stairs and walked into the dark second story room that was The Acropolis club.

A huge room occupied almost the whole of the second story floor. There were tables and chairs by the windows overlooking the street, but all we could see through them was the dark red bricks of the hospital partly obscured by the trees on the other side of Lonsdale Street. Three full size billiard tables occupied most of the room, with dark strip lighting hanging over them at about head height. There were a number of people playing at the tables, dark shadows whose faces only became visible when they leaned forward to make a shot. There were a few people sitting by the windows, sipping coffee and reading newspapers.

"You've just arrived?"

He meant in Australia, not his club.

Even if he hadn't seen us drop our cases at the top of the stairs he would have known we were new arrivals. Our clothes told him that. We were wearing suits, but they were old suits, quite dated I had noticed as we walked along the streets where I could see what other local men were wearing. Everyone I could see in the club was a lot more casually dressed. But apart from that, he knew all his regulars, if not by name, then certainly by face.

He was standing by a small counter near the top of the stairs. Somewhere behind it was a small room where he kept his supplies and the stove on which he boiled the coffee.

"Would you like a coffee? First one is on the house."

I wasn't sure what that meant and looked at him expectantly.

"A free coffee as a welcome to newcomers..." he said.

Ah! We all smiled and nodded. Yes that would be good.

He had a tray with several cups of creamy black Turkish coffee and glasses of water on it.

"Take a seat somewhere, and I'll bring them over. How do you like it?" But before we could answer he said: "Hah, it doesn't matter. I only make them one way, *ghliko*. Saves me worrying about who gets which one. About five minutes, okay?"

"There are a lot of clubs around here," he said when he brought the coffees and the water over, "how did you find out about mine?"

I explained about the two Cretans we met on the ship.

"I think I know who you mean," he said. "They went back about a year ago so they could show all their relatives how rich they were."

"We had to give an address to the immigration people or they wouldn't let us land. Was it all right to give them your's? The Cretans said it was."

"Of course. In fact many people write to their families back home and use this club as their mailing address. I get lots of letters here. Sometimes they sit here a long time."

"What do you do with them?"

"Nothing. I keep them here. Sooner or later the people they are addressed to come and get them. They move around a lot. Take jobs in the country, work a few weeks, come back, and take another job somewhere else. They always come back to find out what's going on, where their friends are, that sort of thing. If you're looking for work, fruit picking is good at the moment, but you'll have to go to Shepparton."

"I don't want to work in the country," I told him. "I'm a tailor. I'd like to work at my own trade."

"There's a man who comes in here sometimes, an Englishman, but he speaks really good Greek. In fact he speaks a number of languages, but he comes in here so he can practice his Greek. He has a friend in the clothing business. Maybe he can help you. I'll introduce you to him next time he's in."

Already things are looking up, I thought.

The proprietor went off to make more coffees for some people seated on the other side of the billiard tables. They were playing backgammon with a lot of enthusiasm, rattling the dice loudly, slamming the tiles down onto the wooden board, almost yelling at each other in their excitement. Someone who didn't understand Greek would have thought they were arguing.

When the proprietor came back, he wanted to know if we had somewhere to stay.

"No," one of my compatriots told him. "We've only just got off the boat."

"Do you know of somewhere?" I asked him.

"Seeing as you are all Epirotics, I can tell by your accent, I feel I can trust you."

"We come from the district of Argyrokastro, which unfortunately is not liberated yet. It is still a part of Albania."

"No matter. All Epirotics are honest and hard workers. I will arrange something. Have another coffee while I go and talk to a friend. I won't be long."

"Well, what do you think?" I asked the others. "Can we trust him?"

"What have we got to lose?" One of them asked.

"We don't have much money, so he can't get that, unless we stay here drinking coffee all day."

"Why don't we see what he does?"

"We've got nothing else to do anyway."

About fifteen minutes later he came back accompanied by an older man with greying hair and shifty eyes, or was that just my imagination?

"This is Mr Stephanos," the proprietor said. "He owns the restaurant down the street. He is an Epirotic too. He is from Yanina."

He shook hands with all of us.

"I've got a large room above the restaurant where you can stay for a few days. I've got some mattresses and pillows, but no beds. I'm sorry I can't accommodate you better. That's the best I can do."

"Sounds good," we said.

"Why don't we go and have a look?"

We followed Mr Stephanos to a couple of buildings further along the street from The Acropolis club and entered through the front of his restaurant.

"You can take your meals here," Mr Stephanos said.

When we protested about not being able to pay for them, he told us not to worry.

"When you get jobs you can pay me back. Epirotics have got to stick together It's the only way we'll win."

We didn't know what to say. We only embarrassed him trying to thank him for his kindness. When he put on his glasses to cover his embarrassment I realised he didn't have shifty eyes at all. He was short sighted and when he wasn't wearing his glasses he tended to squint. I never told him what my first impression was.

***

So we slept on the floor for about two weeks. We didn't care as long as we had somewhere to put our heads.

We were used to hardship.

***

The very next day I bought a newspaper and was sitting in The Acropolis club, drinking coffee and looking through the positions vacant trying to find something that I might be able to do.

There were plenty of jobs advertised in the country. Fruit picking, labouring, that sort of thing, but it was not what I wanted.

Still, if nothing turned up before my money ran out, I would even dig ditches. I was strong enough.

Two of the men with us already had jobs, washing dishes in the restaurant of Mr Stephanos, and in another one that belonged to a friend of his, but it was a start, and they were happy to do that.

Several of the others were leaving on a train for Shepparton in a couple of days. They were going to do fruit picking. That would be hard work, but they had always worked hard, and all of us had worked on farms at one time or another.

But I didn't want to go back to working on a farm. I hadn't come all the way to Australia to do that.

I wanted to do something better. My idea was to start my own business so I would not have to work for someone else, but of course I had to start by working for someone since I had no money.

I looked for a job in the clothing trade but there was nothing like that advertized in the paper.

***

"This is the man I was telling you about," the proprietor of The Acropolis Club said. He had brought a cup of coffee and a glass of water which he placed on the table opposite me. An immaculately dressed elderly gentleman who didn't look the least bit Greek stood by his side.

"He comes here," the proprietor said, "to practice speaking Greek." He introduced us and the man sat down.

We shook hands and he asked me in Greek if I could speak any English.

"Among those who arrived with me the other day," I replied proudly in English ,"I'm the only one."

"Ah, you learnt English in America. How long were you there?"

"Seven years."

"What sort of work did you do? Do you know a trade?"

"I'm a tailor and worked for a year at that trade in America before working as a shirt ironer."

He sipped his coffee and then followed that with a sip of water. Suddenly he stood up. "Come with me," he said.

I followed him to a phone at the back of the club.

"I've a friend who owns a laundry business. Maybe he's got something for you." He dialled a number on the phone mounted to the wall.

He spoke for a few minutes, explaining what I could do. He also said I was willing to learn anything new that I would have to know to work in a laundry, and that as a bonus I could speak excellent English. He listened quietly for a while, then hung up.

"I'm sorry," he said as we returned to our table to finish our coffees. The man I spoke to is a Greek. Unfortunately he doesn't have enough work to warrant employing anyone else at the moment. But don't let that worry you. There's plenty of work out there. You've just got to find it."

Easier said than done, I thought.

"Ah, but you mustn't give up." The man said when he saw the

look of disappointment on my face.

"Of course not."

"In the meanwhile I'll keep a look out. I know a lot of people. I'm sure I'll be able to turn up something you can do."

He finished his coffee which by now was cool enough to swallow in one gulp. He stood up. "I have to go now, but I'll see you soon." And switching into Greek he said, "I promise I'll find something good for you to do."

***

Let's call the man we met in that little shop in Adelaide Spiros. That's a good Greek name.

He was a bit simple, but he was kind hearted. He had one fault though: back home he had been a gambler. He had owned a small restaurant in our village and was a good cook, but he liked to play cards. Sometimes he would win but more often than not he would lose. One night he had too much Ouzo and lost heavily. Like all gamblers he believed that if he kept playing he would eventually win. He started using his restaurant as collateral. He didn't win, and he lost the restaurant. He was so ashamed he stayed drunk for weeks.

All of a sudden he stopped drinking, sobered up and turned to religion asking for forgiveness. But instead of turning to the Greek Orthodox religion like the rest of us, he became a Muslim. He had no real idea other than his belief that Muslims prayed five times a day and faced Mecca while doing so. He started praying at all odd times. Wherever he was, whenever the urge took him he would drop onto his knees, facing where he believed Mecca was, and prayed, bowing, asking Allah for forgiveness. He didn't care if he was in the middle of a group of people or by himself; he would simply drop to his knees and start praying. Anyone nearby would pretend not to see him.

This went on for months, and then suddenly he disappeared. No one knew where he went, but the whole village was relieved because he had become a huge embarrassment. We had heard nothing more about him for such a long time that everyone thought he had died.

Imagine our astonishment to find him working in a shop all the way around the other side of the world in Australia.

He had disappeared quite a few months before we left, and here he was in Adelaide, and obviously happy, established in a job.

Perhaps all those prayers had done some good after all.

For months after our encounter in Adelaide we spoke about him, wondered how he was doing, whether he was still in Adelaide, then gradually we forgot about him until almost twenty years later.

One night I got a phone call from one of my compatriots.

He was very excited. Spiros was in Queensland staying with this Yugoslavian ice cream seller. He wanted to go and get him, and he wanted me to go with him. When I asked why, he said he would explain once we were on our way.

He arrived soon after and we went in his car. On the way he told me that Spiros had been involved in an incident with the police and that they had locked him up.

"What, for twenty years," I asked. "What did he do? Kill someone?"

"No. Nothing like that. They thought he was crazy."

Apparently there is some law up there, a provision in the Queensland Mental Health Act called Article 27A, which permits indefinite incarceration of patients in Psychiatric Institutions.

Spiros went to Queensland to do some sugar cane cutting. He must have arrived at this country station during the night and not having anywhere to go he slept on a bench in the waiting room.

When he woke up in the morning he went out onto the station and laid his prayer mat down and facing North West where he believed Mecca to be he started praying, just like he did back home.

The stationmaster had never seen anything like this before and thought it was rather strange, so he called the police. The police came and saw an unshaven man dressed poorly, kneeling down, bowing continuously and babbling in a strange tongue. they demanded to know what he was doing.

When he ignored them they yelled at him, as if yelling would make him understand English.

He could only speak Greek, and Albanian. He tried to explain to the policemen what he was doing but no one in that town could speak either of those languages; no one knew what poor Spiros was trying to explain, so when they grabbed him he started to struggle with them because he suddenly became frightened.

They decided he must be crazy. They didn't want a crazy man in their jail so they took him to a nearby Asylum.

And there he stayed. They soon found he was a good cook, so they put him to work in the kitchen, cooking the food for the inmates. And that's where he stayed, for years and years.

He wouldn't eat the food, because nearly always it was rotten and flyblown, but the loonies didn't care. They ate it. All Spiros lived on was a little bread and soup, cheese when he could get it, and tea. Once a strong, robust man, he slowly wasted away.

He didn't know how long he was there. He did his work, learnt a few words of English, but hardly enough to talk to anyone, and he prayed. At least they let him do that.

Then one day he heard the sound of a bell in the street outside the high wall of the Asylum exercise yard.

Someone had started riding a bicycle down that street, ringing a bell. It reminded him of the Greek man he had seen in Adelaide selling ice cream on a hot day. He had this tricycle with the two wheels in the front. In between the wheels was a small padded container packed with dry ice where he kept the ice cream.

He would ring a bell to let the kids know he was in the street and they would rush out to buy scoops of ice cream ladled out with a large wooden spoon.

Spiros thought that if this person outside the asylum was an ice cream seller, he might be Greek. So he wrote a message in Greek explaining his situation on a piece of paper and tied it to a stone with some string. It was several days before he heard the man on the bicycle come down the street ringing the bell, and guessing where he might be, he threw the message tied to the stone over the wall.

Well, the man did get the message, but he couldn't read it.

He recognised it as Greek and took it to a cafe owner he knew who translated it for him. They went back together and got Spiros out of the asylum.

Almost twenty years had gone by since that time we saw him in Adelaide.

By this time many Greeks had moved out into the country starting restaurants with names like Athens Cafe or Acropolis Restaurant in the smaller towns. There must have been hundreds of restaurants and fish and chip shops with names like that right across the country.

It was just Spiros' bad luck that when he went to Queensland in the 1920s Greek was not familiar. No one had heard it spoken in country towns away from the major cities so it was unfamiliar. Foreigners who didn't speak or understand English were looked upon with suspicion, especially if they were acting strange.

When we saw poor Spiros we were stunned. We remembered him as being tall and strong, and here facing us was an old, old man; broken and emaciated. He was so happy to see us there were tears in his eyes.

It was not long after coming back to Melbourne that he was diagnosed as having contracted tuberculosis, so he was put in a Sanatorium. God only knows what he thought of that. I believe he simply gave up then...

He never recovered.

***

There was a shop on the other side of the road from Flinders Street railway station where they made lady's clothes.

I'd never done any dressmaking but I thought it wouldn't be too hard to pick up. Making skirts should be a lot easier than making trousers. And if I could make a vest and a suit coat, I ought to be able to make a lady's jacket.

So I went in and asked them for a job. I explained that I was a qualified tailor, and that I had worked as a tailor in America, and on top of that I was very good at pressing shirts.

"Let me show you," I said. Not giving them a chance to protest I went behind the counter and took the steam iron from one of the girls and pressed one of the blouses in the stack she had beside her.

They were certainly surprised, but said they would consider it, and to come back in a day or so and they would give me an answer.

"I don't have much money," I said. "I need to start working as soon as possible."

The person I had spoken to went down the back of the shop to confer with some one whom I couldn't see.

I waited, and watched another girl sewing sleeves onto a jacket. She was using a machine, and the job she did was a bit rough.

I knew I could do better than that by hand, although it was a lot slower. Once they showed me how to use a machine, I would whiz through it. I would turn out heaps of work. Good work. There was no doubt about that.

She came back with a big smile. "The boss says you can start tomorrow."

"That's wonderful."

"But only on condition."

"What condition?"

"That you can do the same kind of work we are. It's just a try out."

"Sounds good to me. What time do you start?"

"Eight o'clock."

"I'll be here."

"Hey," the girl called out as I was going out the front door. "I like your American accent."

***

"Life is full of choices," the old man said one Sunday.

He was holding the small copper and brass coffee pot over the gas ring. He would raise it as the coffee started to boil, the thick dark cream frothing as it almost boiled over. As the creamy head subsided he would lower the pot to let the coffee start boiling a second time. It would boil much quicker the second time and the instant it reached the top of the tiny pot he would lift it off and quickly pour the thick black coffee into two small cups.

There is nothing quite like the smell of freshly boiled Turkish coffee. Its aroma filled the kitchen with the memories of a thousand Kafeneions and Tavernas.

"The only good thing the Turks ever did," he often said during these Sunday morning conversations, "was to teach us how to make coffee."

He put the two cups of coffee on the table and beside each he placed a glass of cold water. From his glass he meticulously allowed one tiny drop of water to fall into his coffee. "To settle grains," he explained as he watched that drop puncture a tiny hole in the centre of the creamy surface.

"I wonder," he said after taking his first careful sip of the hot coffee, "what my life in Australia would have been like if I had taken that first job."

***

A Sunday morning conversation with Dad and Mum... circa 1964.

***

We were lucky.

When we arrived there were thousands of people unemployed in Melbourne. Of course it was nothing like it is now. But it was harder then.

If you didn't have a job, there was no dole. You depended on the charity of friends, or the Church.

Yeah, I think we were lucky. Within two weeks all of us had found some kind of work, even if it was only washing dishes.

***

I was ecstatic.

I couldn't wait to get back to the club to tell the others I had found a job.

I started to run back along Swanston Street.

89

I almost ran all the way back in my excitement, then suddenly, while waiting for the lights at the corner of Swanston and Lonsdale streets to change so I could cross, I began to get nervous.

What if I had lost my skill with the needle?

It's been ten years since I did any sewing, since I had made a suit, or even part of a suit. All that time in America, apart from the first year, I had been pressing shirts. And back home, it was farm work. No one in my village could afford to have a suit made. All I had done there was to help my mother repair our own clothes as needed.

Worrying about this I slowed down to a walk as I crossed over and entered Lonsdale Street.

I failed to see one of my compatriots coming along the footpath towards me.

"Hey why so glum?" he asked as he stopped in front of me. I was so preoccupied I almost bumped into him.

"I think I've got a job."

"And that's why you look glum?"

"No, of course not. I'm worried about whether I'll be able to do it well enough. It's only a test. If they like what I do I'll get it, if not...."

"Don't worry about it. Just do it."

He took hold of my shoulder. "That English man you met the other day is in the club looking for you."

"Thanks."

I ran the rest of the way to the Acropolis club, pausing at the entrance to catch my breath, before walking steadily up the stairs to the second floor.

"What's up?" the man selling dried fruits and nuts spread out on a small wooden box beside the entrance to the club asked.

"I've got a job."

"Don't drop dead before you start," he said.

Upstairs my English friend came over to me as soon as he saw me come in. "I've organised a job for you," he said with a big grin.

"It's a good job, you'll like it. But you will have to go to Mildura."

Well, I didn't know what to say. I just sat there and stared at him while he explained it all to me.

"A friend of mine is opening a new dry cleaning factory in Mildura and he needs someone to work as a presser. You would also do minor alterations as well. I didn't want to say anything before until I had spoken to him about you. You seem to be made for this job. You speak English, you're a qualified tailor, and you've had experience at pressing. All you need to do now is to learn how to use the dry cleaning machinery, to do the cleaning."

The more he talked the more excited I got.

"They are still installing the factory," he said, "and they would like you to go there so you can tell them the best place to put each machine."

"But I don't know anything about how to set up a factory like that."

"It doesn't matter. You soon will."

"I don't understand."

"I've arranged for you to spend a week at a dry cleaning factory in Richmond, starting tomorrow. This is the fellow I spoke to the other day, who doesn't have enough work to enable him to employ you. But he is quite willing to let you come over for few days so he can teach you how everything works, how you set up the machines, how to deal with the customers, that sort of thing."

"It sounds too good to be true."

"There's more yet. Since you'll in effect be running the place, the more business you do the more you'll earn. You'll get ten percent, when you start making a profit, apart from your wages which I believe will be ten pounds a week."

This was absolutely terrific. I could not have wished for a better deal. Then suddenly I remembered that I had just accepted a job, and that I was to start it tomorrow. What was I going to do now? I couldn't go back on my word. I had already told them I would be there at eight o'clock in the morning.

When I explained this his advice was: "You have to make a choice."

"If I was you I'd go to Mildura. Forget the other job. With the money you save by working in the country you will one day be able to start your own business. But of course it's up to you. It's your choice."

Start my own business! That was something I dreamed about but didn't really consider a possibility. But when I heard him say that the idea started growing in my mind, and it did seem possible. This was a vibrant new country and enything at all was possible, even me owning my own business. Other Greeks coming to Australia had done it before, so why not me, or any of the others who came with me?

"I'll have to go back to that tailor's shop in Flinders street and tell them I've found something better," I said. "If I don't, when I don't show up tomorrow morning they are going to think Greeks are a rotten lot, and that you can't trust them."

"And you wouldn't want them to think that."

"Well, certainly not about Greeks from Epirus," I said.

Mr Cassidy laughed.

Suddenly I realised that I had made my choice.

***

I met the man who was opening the dry cleaning plant in Mildura. He was staying at the Windsor Hotel, a beautiful old Hotel, very elegant. I felt out of place but he assured me that I was fine. We had tea and some home made sweet bread he called scones which I thought were very nice. I didn't have them with cream and jelly, but with butter which melted into them because the scones were hot.

We got on very well together and I couldn't wait to start working for him.

"You already are," he told me; "from tomorrow anyway. Even though you'll be working for a few days with my associate in Richmond, at his dry cleaning plant, it will be me who pays you. He will teach you how to operate the cleaning and spotting. Pressing I presume you already know."

"Yes. Trousers, shirts and jackets, of course."

"Good. My friend Oscar, at Richmond will teach you whatever else you need to know. In fact his son, who you will meet there is coming with you to Mildura. The two of you will work together. Mr Oscar's father is the engineer who will set up the machinery we need in the factory. I will see you all in Mildura next week."

I assumed we would be going to Mildura by train. It wasn't until I started working at Mr Oscar's factory that I found out we were going to fly to Mildura.

That would be something new. I had never been in a plane before. I was looking forward to it.

***

"Never again," I vowed once we got to Mildura.

I'll never forget that plane ride.

I had thought travelling in a plane was like travelling in a bus. I never imagined that being in the air was worse than being on the water.

I was quite happy until it took off. Right at the end of the runway it made a sideways lurch that made me queasy, and then as it got higher it sort of floated up and down just like a boat. Worse than a boat...

"Keep your seat belt on," Harry said. Harry was Mr Oscar's son. He had the window seat, and I was glad because I didn't want to look out and see how far up we were.

"Why?"

"Because the hostess told me we would hit a lot of turbulence today."

Before I could comment on that the plane suddenly dropped out from beneath us. My stomach flew up into my throat, and I couldn't breathe.

The whole plane shuddered like a truck running over a lot of corrugations in the road, and then it shot back up again. We were pushed down into our seats.

I couldn't say anything. I knew if I opened my mouth I would vomit. I could feel the saliva welling up in my mouth.

Suddenly there was a hostess standing beside me, a concerned expression on her face. She handed me a heavy brown paper bag. "If you feel sick, you can use this," she said. "Is this your first time in a plane?"

I nodded.

"It's not always as bad as this," she said. "Please don't feel embarrassed."

Harry took no notice of me. He was enjoying himself, staring out the window, watching the countryside pass below.

I vomited as quietly as possible into the paper bag.

After a while the hostess came and took it off me. She gave me another bag but there was nothing left to bring up. Even so I couldn't stop myself from retching violently.

Every time the plane moved up or down, or wobbled sideways, my stomach heaved.

Although the flight was only an hour and a bit, it seemed to last forever.

***

My first three months in Mildura flew past so quickly I hardly noticed them. We were so busy we often had to work overtime.

Work and sleep, that's all I did.

I slept in a room at the back of the shop so I saved a lot of money on rent.

When I had enough to exchange for fifty American Dollars I sent the money to Mr Cassidy in Melbourne and he obtained a bank draft for me and sent it to my family in Albania. It was of course for my wife and daughter. I was determined to support them in a manner befitting a person of good means.

Things settled down after the first three months and I had some free time. I wrote letters home but never got any replies, so I never knew if they got the money I had Mr Cassidy send to them.

So when I had more saved up I sent it in cash, ten US dollars at a time.

There was a good chance the letters would be opened when they arrived in Albania and the money stolen, but on the other hand the odd small amount of money might get to them whereas a bank draft for a large amount would certainly get stolen. It was well known that people in the post office opened the mail coming in. Their reason was they didn't want local people in Albania to find out how much better life was elsewhere. They wanted to stop people leaving. Of course if there was any money in a letter they would appropriate it for themselves and not forward the letter on.

My hope was that they couldn't open every letter that came into the country from all over the world. Some of the mail would have to get through intact. Even if I lost ten dollars from time to time, some of it would get through to my wife.

I also had time to look around the town and decided Mildura was too small a town for me.

I wrote to Mr Cassidy and asked him to keep an eye out for a suitable place I could use to set up my own business, and he said he would do that. He also said to stick with the job I had because the pay was good. It would take quite a bit of money to set up your own business, so while I was in Mildura, where there were no distractions and nothing to spend money on, it was a good place to save.

He sent me a list of prices for cleaning and pressing machines and he was right, there was no way I could have afforded to buy any of that stuff. I would have to be patient and wait a bit longer.

***

I was so excited when my first letter came from Albania. It had been sent to the Acropolis Club and Mr Cassidy had forwarded it to me in Mildura.

But the news was upsetting.

The letter was from my father and he informed me that my brother George had been taken by the authorities and imprisoned. He had been sentenced to do hard labour in lieu of Christos whom they claimed was a spy for the Greeks.

Christos had gone over the mountains into Greece for medical treatment. When he came back and went to the police with his medical papers and proof of treatment, George was released. But there was never a word of apology from the authorities, just a warning that it better not happen again. This was the last straw as far as George was concerned. Having fought for freedom he was again a prisoner in his own land.

After leaving America, George had gone back to Greece where he volunteered for the Greek army.

He took part in several battles that helped liberate Northern Epirus only to find when the First World War ended and after the Italians had gone the part of Epirus where we were born was again handed over to the Albanians and conditions for Epirotic Greeks trapped over the border became worse.

I wrote and suggested that he should come to Australia. I told him it was truly a free country, and since he had tasted freedom in America, he would love it here. He had been reluctant to leave when I had because he had a family with his eldest son sixteen years old. Whereas I had only one child. It was easier for me to leave than it was for him. It would also be easier for me to bring out my family when the time came than it would be for him.

I knew Christos would never leave his sheep and his beloved mountains, and that despite the restrictions imposed by the Albanian authorities, he was happy there.

I sent George some money and told him to put it towards the fare to Australia, and that when I could I would send more.

There was no word about my wife or daughter, which was very strange, since I asked about them in every letter I sent home.

***

Spiro with a friend somewhere near Mildura circa 1927...

I was more determined than ever to start my own business after two and a half years in Mildura, so I told the people with whom I was working that I wanted to leave, but I would stay until they got a replacement. I would of course stay long enough to teach my replacement whatever was needed to do the job properly.

"When you get back to Melbourne," Harry said, "see my Dad and he'll help you. He'll probably give you a job."

I didn't know what to say. I didn't want to ask Mr Oscar for a job. In fact I knew I wouldn't. I had enough money saved up to keep me going for a while, so when I got to Melbourne I would have time to look around, not like the last time when I had to get a job straight away just to survive. Besides, I was missing my friends and was curious to know how they were getting on.

Also, over the last two years I had been sending money to George and he now had enough money to pay for his fare to Australia. Though he hadn't written to me yet, I knew he would come soon. I could feel it.

I couldn't wait to see him. I desperately wanted to know what was going on at home.

In the few letters I had received, no one ever said much except to thank me for the money, that they were in good health, and that they send their regards.

Useless words!

Words that told me nothing.

***

The Acropolis club hadn't changed. It was still dark and smoky inside, and the smell of strong Turkish coffee being brewed filled my lungs with the scent of home. The sharp smack of a cue hitting a billiard ball punctuated the murmur of voices from the people seated at the tables.

Of course I went there first. It was the only place in Melbourne where I felt at home. It was also the only place where I was likely to bump into one of my friends, or at least to find out how they were getting on. But there was no one there I recognised apart from the owner.

"How was Mildura?" he asked as I stood beside the counter that separated the space where he made the coffees from the rest of the club.

He was good with faces. He never forgot anyone.

"You were one of the lucky ones," he said.

I wasn't sure what he meant so I said nothing.

"Getting a good job so soon after arriving," he added. He gestured towards a loud group playing billiards in the far corner. A pall of cigarette smoke filled the corner and there was a lot of yelling and gesticulating. "Those men haven't seen work for months. Probably don't even know what the word means anymore."

I laughed. "Maybe they were just unlucky."

"Lazy, that's all," he said as he turned back to put a freshly prepared kafechi on the gas ring.

A moment later he lifted the kafechi from the gas ring and poured the still bubbling coffee into a small cup. He pushed it towards me.

"Just the way you like it," he said.

Of course he only made it one way, so that was the way everyone liked it.

He gave me a glass of ice water, and I tipped a drop into my cup to settle the grains.

I sat there a long time savouring the coffee but no one I knew came in, so I went out to buy a newspaper. I needed to look for a place to live. I also wanted to rent a room for my brother George who I was sure was on his way from Greece and would be here soon.

***

Not long after I had got back to Melbourne a letter came from George to tell me that he was on his way. I was so happy I didn't know how to express myself. I ran around telling everyone my brother was on his way and would soon be here.

They said, "That's nice," then went on with whatever they were doing. They couldn't have cared less.

But I cared. It had been so long since I had seen anyone from my own family, I couldn't wait. What George didn't tell me in his letter was that his eldest son, Michal, was coming with him.

***

I was there when the ship docked, and when George and his eldest son came anxiously down the gangplank I was so excited I rushed up to them and hugged and kissed them. There were tears in my eyes, and lots of Australians who worked in the area looked at me rather strangely, but I didn't care. I was so happy to see someone from my own family after all the time I had been in Australia.

I was not to know then that hardly anyone else would ever come, that the border would once again be closed and that those Greeks and Albanians who lived in Albania would be kept as prisoners in their own country. I could never have imagined that the Government would use forced labour to build fortifications around the country not to keep invaders out as they claimed; but to keep their own people in. This came after the Second World War and was so far in the future as to be unimaginable. I was just so happy to see my brother and his son.

***

George, as he looked on arrival in Melbourne in 1927.

As soon as they arrived George tried to get a job as a tanner. That's what he said he did best. That was what he did in America when we went there together. On his first trip there he had worked in a textile mill, and of course at home he worked the flour mill as well as being a farmer. He had much more experience in the workforce that I had, and could turn his hand to anything.

Unfortunately there were no jobs for tanners available in Melbourne. It was towards the end of 1927 and it was a struggle getting any kind of work. I had taken a job as a presser once again with Mr Oscar at Richmond who really didn't need any extra pressers and only employed me out of the kindness of his heart.

I had made a number of friends and one of them owned as small restaurant in Russell Street. They served three course meals at a reasonable price and were always busy. He was a Greek and knew how hard it was to get started in a foreign country so he agreed to take on my brother as an assistant when I asked him. Not only that, he knew of a barbershop nearby where my nephew could also get a job.

So in no time at all they were both working and things were looking better.

***

When the letter arrived from home I tore it open as anxiously as I had any other letter, happy to receive news from home.

We were in the Acropolis Club, George and I, drinking our usual coffees. The place was crowded and noisy and filled with smoke.

"What's the matter?" George asked when he saw what must have been a stunned look on my face.

"Can you believe this?" I threw the letter on the table and he quickly snatched it up and read it.

It was not a long letter, only one page, but it said that my wife was using the money I had been sending her to run around and have a good time with another man. She had left my daughter with our mother and had gone off with this other man. It didn't say who this other man was, nor did it say who wrote the letter. It certainly wasn't my mother's or my father's hand writing. In fact it was hardly legible, as if the person writing it didn't have good control of his hand.

"Do you know anything about this?" I asked George.

He looked evasive. "No," he said, as he refolded the letter and put it back in the envelope. "I don't know anything about this."

"You have no idea who wrote this letter?"

He shook his his head as he said "No."

I didn't believe him.

"You were there. You must have seen or heard something. Did she go out with some other man?"

"I never saw her do that."

"What about my daughter?"

"Well of course she left her with our mother. What else was she going to do when there was work to be done?"

"Did you ever hear of her going out with some other man?"

"No," George said again, this time angrily because it was not something he wanted to talk about. "I never saw her go out with anyone, and I never heard of it either. Now are you satisfied?"

"Then why would someone write a letter like this?" I picked up the letter and waved it in front of his face.

He couldn't answer that. He just stood up and said, "My coffee is cold. I'm going to get another one."

I stuffed the letter in my pocket and went outside.

It was windy and wild and the trees in front of the hospital over the road from the club writhed furiously. Dust blew along the street making my eyes sting. I threw the letter into a rubbish bin on the corner of Lonsdale and Russell Streets.

After a while I pulled out the pictures George had given me when he arrived. They were of my daughter Verga, one taken with our Mother. The other taken by herself at a different time.

I couldn't believe how much she had grown.

I stared at those pictures for a long time and finally vowed that I would do whatever it took to get Verga to come to Australia.

***

***

There was often bad feelings in those villages along the Albanian side of the Greek border. For almost 500 years they had been slaves working for the benefit of the Ottoman Empire, and then when freedom came it was short-lived and the people in those villages, because they were Greek and a minority, were treated badly by the Albanians. There was no work for them other than the most menial, their language was forbidden except at home, so they took out their frustration and anger upon each other.

There were many who stayed in the villages because they lacked the courage to go out into the world, or who were unable to leave for other reasons. They were always jealous of those who had managed to leave to become successful enough in foreign countries to send money home. The families that received this money were often the recipients of slander and innuendo, of lies and stories spread around to discredit them.

Letters filled with lies about what was happening to people in all the villages were written to the young men overseas. Lies about what the young men overseas were doing were spread around the villages.

That the people to whom these lies were directed believed them was unfortunate, but they believed them because they came from people they trusted, people they knew and thought were friends.

In the case of the old man, someone wrote and told him his wife was having a good time using the money he sent over to her to run around with some man in the next village. Someone who didn't sign his name and was forever unidentified.

He was so upset about this he immediately stopped sending money.

No doubt the same people told his wife that her husband had found another woman in Australia and was no longer interested in her.

Neither story was true but both of them believed it.

After long delays because dealing with government officials in Albania by mail from Australia was almost impossible, he arranged for a divorce.

And much later he did find someone else and he remarried.

While over there no doubt, like most of the women left without money and waiting for husbands to send for them, she eventually found another man. What else could she have done?

Both were victims of circumstances and events beyond their control.

***

A few months after George started work in the kitchen I said to him: "Now that you know all about cooking, what about starting something of your own?"

He stared at me as if I had said sosmething strange, but to me this was obviously what we had to do.

Working for other people was good, but you never got far.

I had looked around and seen what my compatriots from the boat were doing and it was all menial work, cleanaing floors in office buildings, washing dishes in kitchens like Theo did...

Theo was the young man who had helped all of us who were sea-sick on the way over. How we had envied him for never getting sick. But here he was washing dishes. And Nick who had trouble speaking English could only find work cleaning up the mess in an abattoir, or when he wasn't doing that, digging ditches along a roadside. Sadly he drank too much beer for his own good, but who could blame him?

And what about George? Was he anything more than a dish washer and an assitant cook? At least he had learned how to cook. And me, I wanted to start my own business too, but I didn't have enough money. None of us did, even though we saved as much as we could.

"Well, what do you think?" George asked. "Can we do it?"

"Of course we can, if we pool our resources."

Perhaps I was too optimistic.

"You know how to cook," I said. "Theo can run the kitchen. He's worked in kitchens for two years now. My English is good so I can talk to people. I'll wait on tables. I don't mind doing that. Between the three of us it should be no problem."

"Then we'll do it," George's eyes glowed enthusiastically.

What amazing confidence we had in ourselves!

We were young. We were full of energy. We didn't mind hard work or long hours. Perhaps we were overconfident, even a little foolish, but we were convinced that the only way to improve our lot was to make our own work by starting our own businesses.

A lot of migrants had done just that, and they were prosperous. It was people like that who had employed us because they knew how difficult it was to get anything but the poorest of jobs.

But not everyone was like that. We didn't look at the many who stayed as labourers or factory workers. Most of them worked hard and saved their money to eventually buy a house, to marry and to raise chidlren.

There were some who had been here longer than us and still hardly spoke a word of English. A few even refused to learn English and stayed within their own group doing nothing but complain about how hard it was to get anywhere. We didn't listen to their grumbles and dissatisfactions, or their longing to return home to something familiar rather than trying to accommodate themselves to a new life in a new land. We had nothing in common with them other than our mother tongue.

But most importantly, there was no one to tell us we couldn't do what we wanted to do, so we simply went ahead and did it.

Instead of renting an empty shop and creating a restaurant, we found a small already established business in Elizabeth Street that was for sale and we bought that.

We paid a deposit in cash and signed an agreement to pay the balance in monthly instalments over a year. The owner of the restaurant stayed with us for a few weeks to teach us how he ran his business, as well as to introduce us to his regular customers.

After that we were on our own.

***

"We should get Christos to come over and join us," George said one night after we had closed the shop and were cleaning up in the kitchen.

"You'd never get him to come here," I said. "He would be lost here. How long did he stay in America when he went there with you the first time? Two months? Three? He missed his sheep. He knows every one of those sheep by sight, probably even has a name for each one of them. He'd never leave them."

"I suppose you're right," George said. "I just thought it would be nice if we were all here together."

"You know," I said to Theo, "that you could take half a dozen of Christos' sheep and stick them in a flock of a thousand, and he could walk in amongst those sheep and, without a mistake, pick his own ones out. I couldn't tell one from another, they all look the same to me."

"There isn't another shepherd like Christos in the whole country," George said. "His only trouble is he lacks ambition."

"No, he's happy where he is. It's what he wants to do. He went to America. He didn't like it. He went home and he loves it.

He's different from us, that's all."

***

George must have been a good cook because in no time business picked up and we were doing quite well. We even had to hire a waitress to assist us. People used to say George cooked the best steaks in town, and I used to joke with them, telling them that it was George's experience as a tanner in America that made him so good at cooking steaks. Some of them gave me odd looks, not sure if I was being serious because I always said this with a straight face. Many just nodded and accepted what I'd said. I think they actually believed me.

One night, my English friend Mr Cassidy came in for a cup of coffee and Mr Oscar accompanied him. I thought something was up when I saw them enter but once Mr Cassidy asked me if I was still interested in starting a dry cleaning business I was sure of it.

I had to think about it for a moment, not because I didn't want to do it, but because I had committed myself to being a partner in the restaurant with George and Theo. I enjoyed the work and the interaction with the customers, but it was not what I was trained to do. Finally I had to say "Yes," unequivocally.

"Good, then I've found the right suburb for you." Mr Cassidy said. "There's no dry cleaner there other than a small agent. And he shouldn't bother you once you get started."

"There is a laundry there," Mr Oscar said, "but they don't do dry cleaning. And you don't have to worry about setting up a plant until you can afford it. Just bundle up the stuff to be cleaned and send it to me by train. When it's cleaned I'll send it back to you and all you have to do it press it."

Even though I owned part of the restaurant with George and Theo the clothing trade was my game, and I now realised that the sooner I could get back to it the happier I would be.

"What about George and Theo and the restaurant? I just can't walk out and leave them. We started this together."

"Talk to them. They'll understand."

***

Mr Cassidy and I went to Williamstown and after walking from The Strand up along Ferguson Street we came to a vacant shop in a small group of shops almost opposite the picture theatre.

It was just perfect. With Mr Oscar to do the cleaning, all I had to do was buy a steam iron for the pressing and I could start.

I knew an Armenian Greek who was a carpenter. I could hire him to come and fit out the shop with counters and benches, shelves and cupboards. I would also do hats, reblocking, and any repairs to garments would be no problem at all since I was a qualified tailor.

All kinds of ideas were running through my head when Mr Cassidy asked, "Well, what do you think?"

"I think you are looking at the man who just started his own Dry Cleaning business."

I couldn't stop smiling.

"That's great." Mr Cassidy slapped me on the back. Let's go and see the Estate Agent and you can sign the lease.

A few days I registered the business name and organised the carpenter to make the counters. Once that was done I opened the door to the public for the first time. It was almost four years since I had arrived.

***

Not long after that my nephew whom everyone now called Mick instead of Mihal started his own Barber shop in Russell Street.

It was a small shop beside a tiny lane that gave access to the rear of a row of small shops. That meant the three of us, George, myself, and Mick had all started our own businesses; within a few years of us having arrived in Australia: quite an achievement for a bunch of boys from a small village in Northern Greece!

***

I put a sign in the window the day I opened the door for the first time.

I drew a word in the shape of clouds. Everyone who saw the sign knew what I was referring to, because, like me they had all run out into the street to watch the word appear in the sky.

We all stood out in the open and stared up at the sky watching this tiny little silver speck trailing a long thin cloud.

No one said anything at first. They just stared up in wonder at the thought that someone, a human being was actually creating clouds artificially.

The tiny aeroplane had made two parallel lines of cloud. At the end of the second line the plane disappeared and it was quite a while before we saw it again. We could hear it though, a throbbing sound from its motor. It was so high up we couldn't see until a flash of sunlight glinting off a wing pinpointed it for us as it approached the two lines at right angles. It made another line across the middle to spell the letter H.

When the plane started another long line someone stated the obvious: "It's writing — writing in the sky!"

That is exactly what it was doing, making artificial clouds and using them to write a word in the sky.

So I made a sign on a big sheet of paper. I wanted to introduce myself to the people of Williamstown. I put the sign in the window where everyone could see it. I drew it with big fluffy letters so no one would mistake the reference

The sign said: HELLO.

***

What got people in at first, was the fact that I cleaned and rejuvenated hats. Hardly anyone did this. Certainly no dry cleaning agents did. Not even Mr Oscar did hats. When he got one he would bring it to me to do, but he only did this when he had enough to warrant a trip from Richmond to Williamstown. So the service he offered was at least a week, whereas I could do the hats and have them ready the next day.

In the twenties and thirties every man wore a hat so it wasn't long before I was inundated with hats to be cleaned.

I bought a binding machine with a ten pound deposit and six monthly instalments to pay it off. That was essential for replacing the binding around the edge of the hat brim. I also managed to obtain a set of blocks, or wooden moulds in various sizes, which I needed to reshape the hats after they had been cleaned. When each hat was finished I put it in the window on a little stand so people could see what a good job I did. There were always five or six hats in the window.

When I wasn't doing hats it seemed I was always carrying bundles of clothes parcelled in canvas bags to the North Williamstown railway station. They went to North Richmond where Mr Oscar would collect them and clean them for me in his factory. He would send them back the next day and I would press them with a hand steam iron the way I had been taught to do as a tailor. It was time consuming and tedious. I wished I had enough money to buy a small boiler and a proper steam utility press. With that equipment I would get through the pressing ten times as fast.

Still I had to start somewhere, and though the hours were long, I was very happy to be working for myself. I didn't care how long I worked. I kept going until everything was finished so I could start each day fresh without having to catch up with leftover jobs from the day before.

I worked and saved every penny, only going to The Acropolis Club once a week for a decent coffee and a chat with my compatriots to see what they were up to.

***

When it was time to renew the lease I decided I would be better off around the corner in Douglas Parade. There were more shops there, and more people. It was a much busier street than the part of Ferguson Street where I had my little shop.

A shop not much bigger than the one I was already in had become vacant so I quickly I took up the lease. It was at number 11 Douglas Parade, the last of a row of shops extending from the Ferguson Street corner.

I bought a dry cleaning machine and a small boiler to supply steam for a utility press.

This was an important move because with my own plant I could do all the work and be totally independent. No more relying on the goodwill of others. Even though I paid Mr Oscar for his cleaning services I'm sure he didn't make much out of it, and the sooner I could do my own work, the better it would be for both of us.

But most importantly, I looked forward to the day when I didn't have to walk to that blasted station carrying bags of clothes over my shoulder. That would be terrific.

***

It was wild and stormy the night they took me out to talk to the Greek ship's Captain.

The Second World War had been raging across Europe and the Japanese had entered the conflict by attacking and occupying most of South East Asia. Singapore had fallen and the Japanese had already attacked Darwin and other towns in the far North. A line had been drawn across Australia from the East coast to the West coast and the Government was prepared to abandon that part of the country should the Japanese invade, and it looked very much like they might do just that. A mini-sub had been blown up in Sydney Harbour after it had attacked some ships, and there was talk that a big submarine had been seen along the Victorian coast.

Two men, officers from the Army, came and banged on the door a bit after midnight one night. One of them I knew because he was a customer and I often had his uniform in the shop for cleaning and pressing. The other one was a stranger.

When they told me they wanted me to go out onto a ship and talk to the Captain, I said: "No way. I'm not getting onto any ship in weather like this."

A ferocious wind blew along Douglas Parade pushing waves of rain before it. A big V sign on the shop over the road from us shivered and swayed, looking as if it was about to be blown over. This was not a night to go out, let alone go down to the harbour to go on board a ship. I hated ships and the sea because every time I had ever been on one I got horribly sick.

"The ship is already here in Port Melbourne. We need you to translate. The captain hardly speaks any English."

"Why me?"

"Because you're the only Greek person I know," the man I knew said. "Look, the ship has just come over from Perth and the captain claims he saw something he thought was a submarine in Bass Strait. That's all we can get out of him. No one on the ship speaks any English, so we need some help. The only person I could think of was you."

I couldn't very well refuse; after all this was my country now. "Let me get dressed and I'll be right there."

The weather didn't get any better as we drove along Douglas Parade. There were tree branches scattered all along the road and sheets of rain sometimes blocked the driver's view ahead and he was forced to slow down to a crawl. No one said much of anything during the slow drive to Port Melbourne. We had to go the long way around because the ferry didn't run at this time of night. In any case it certainly wouldn't be crossing the river in weather like this even if it was operating. There were hardly any streetlights on and the driver used only his parking lights to maintain some semblance of blackout, so it was very dark. By contrast there were lights all over the Greek ship when we pulled up next to the gang-plank on the wharf.

The Captain looked tired and haggard. He had been smoking a lot and there were ashtrays full of butts all over the table.

There were also several empty coffee cups, a number of charts of Bass Strait, and several pages of notepaper with scribbled drawings on them.

"Are you the translator?" The Captain asked with a cracked husky voice. He spoke to me in Greek. The man he been studying a chart with looked up as we walked in. He was wearing a Naval Officer's uniform.

"Yes," I answered the Captain in formal Greek.

"Good," the Naval Officer said. "How's your English?"

"As good as yours," I told him.

"You're an American." My accent had surprised him.

"No, I'm a Greek," I said, and didn't elaborate.

Then the Captain started to tell me what he had seen. He was convinced it had been a submarine, a very big one. Judging by the length, he estimated it must have been about two thousand tons.

But it had been twilight and the weather was not the best. Before he could get too close to it, the submarine submerged.

"That's not possible," the Army officer said.

"Why not?" I asked on behalf of the Captain.

"Because that would make it as big or bigger than our Oberon Class submarines."

"How do you know it was a submarine?" I asked the Captain.

"Because I saw submarines in Europe. I know what they look like. Besides, it submerged before we could get close enough to get a good look."

"It is possible," the Navy man said quietly.

We turned to look at him.

"The Japanese have a couple of very large ones. I don't know what they call them, but they are big, two thousand six hundred tons perhaps. The Americans have seen them in the Pacific. It's just possible one of them might have come down here to reconnoitre the coast, to check our defences. This can't be overlooked. If there is one here," and he pointed to the chart of Bass Strait indicating a spot somewhere near Apollo Bay, "then we'll have to find it and destroy it."

They got me to ask the Captain a few more questions about the exact location where he saw the submarine. Then they thanked me and asked me not to tell anyone about what we had discussed, and took me home.

It was late, I was tired, and there was a lot of work to do the next morning. I fell into bed and went to sleep almost immediately.

It was years later when I found there actually had been a Japanese submarine out there. The RAAF spent two weeks flying over Bass Strait looking for it and couldn't find it.

That submarine did carry a spy plane that was used to fly over Melbourne and Williamstown. The people manning the anti aircraft guns on the rifle range saw it. They thought it was Japanese by its markings but before they could shoot at it they had to get permission from headquarters and by the time that happened it was gone.

It was a bit farcical when you think about it.

The plane even flew over the Laverton air base and no one took any notice of it. It flew over Williamstown and Port Melbourne, and probably made a ccircuit around the Melbourne itself before heading back to Bass Strait and its mother ship.

What if it had carried bombs and had dropped them on the city? What would we have done then?

A few weeks later the nervous gunners on the rifle range tried to shoot down an American plane thinking it was another Japanese one.

Fortunately they missed.

***

I suppose it's ironic, but I became one of those people that back in the village we used to wonder about.

I became one of those who stopped writing and sending money home.

I was so angry when I heard that my wife was using the money to have a goot time running around with another man; a cousin no less.

There was no way I was going to send the money I worked so hard for over to her to spend in such a frivolous way.

I cut myself off completely. I didn't even write to my parents. I simply concentrated on my work and tried to forget about everything over there.

But George kept in touch. Apart from Mick who was his eldest and only son in Australia, he had several children and his wife still there in Dervitsani. He was always sending money to his wife. He would change Australian pounds for American dollars and send her the dollars since that was the only foreign currency that people over there accepted. He also wrote to our parents and kept them informed about me and what I was doing, so I suppose to them, I didn't really disappear like some of the others had.

***

It's funny how you meet people, and your life changes.

I'd been working on my own for a couple of years and could have done with some help but I was reluctant to hire anyone because I wasn't making that much money. It was still a struggle. Everyone was still trying to cope with the depression the whole world had suffered. But Australia wasn't as bad as Europe. It looked very much like there was going to be a war there again.

Then one night I went to George's cafe just to talk to him and the others. I often went there, because after all George was my only family here and the other people in the kitchen were my friends and compatriots. We had shared the journey to Australia together and always had lots to talk about.

This particular night I discovered a new waitress. She was cheerful and friendly with blonde hair and sparkling eyes.

She'd only been there a couple of days but didn't seem the least bit nervous. She chatted to the customers as they sat down to order and she was quick on her feet. She was very Australian. I liked her.

In fact I liked her so much I asked her to go out with me after she finished work.

She turned me down, telling me: "I don't go out with foreigners."

"Why not?" I asked innocently. "What's wrong with foreigners?"

"Ah, you know. I mean your English isn't bad, but some of the men who ask me out can hardly speak any English. They're only after one thing," she said bluntly, "and I'm not gonna do that."

I went red in the face. I could feel the blush burning my cheeks. For a moment I didn't know what to say. In my country a woman doesn't talk like that to a man she's just met.

George, standing nearby, heard the conversation. I could see his eyes sparkle but he said nothing.

A voice behind me said, "I'll go out with you."

I turned around to find another young lady who looked very much like the waitress, only she had brown hair and was slightly chubbier. She also had a very nice smile.

"I'll go out with anybody if they take me to dinner," she joked.

That put me on the spot. What could I do except ask her if she'd like to come out with me the next night?

"I like foreigners," she said. "I like Greek. I think it has such a lovely sound to it."

"Meet my sister," said the waitress. "Her name's Mary."

Then she rushed off to take someone's order leaving the two of us standing in the middle of the restaurant.

"Well?" Mary asked.

"Well what?" I asked awkwardly.

"Are you going to ask me?"

"Do you want to go out to dinner tomorrow night?" I blurted.

"I'd love to."

And that was that. Suddenly I relaxed. I was no loger awkward. We chose a time and a place to meet the next evening, and after that she was off, calling out cheerfully as she went out the front door: "See you tomorrow then."

George shook his head and smiled when I went back into the kitchen. He had seen and heard it all.

"I think you'd better make me a coffee," I said, to hide my embarrassment, but at the same time I was excited about the prospect of going out with a young lady. It was something I had never really done before.

"You know what?" I said to George, "She didn't even ask me my name."

George just shrugged as he passed me the coffee he had made.

I was not to know then that this delightfully forward young lady would later become my wife.

***

Mary in the mid 1930s

As it turned out, Mary didn't have a job and no money either. She was sharing a room in Fitzroy with her sister who worked for George, and used to come around to the restaurant to collect some left overs to take home to eat.

She'd had a hard life because her mother died while she was quite young. Her father married the housekeeper who became the stepmother. The stepmother was all sweetness while her father was around, but when he was at work she made life miserable for the two girls, who eventually were forced to leave home to find work, and some other place to live. Not only did they have to leave home which was a country town in New South Wales called Cobar; because there was no work there for young girls they headed to Melbourne where work in a large city was more likely to be found.

They had rented a room in a pub in Fitzroy, and Mary helped the owners doing kitchen work and minding the kids for a few shillings a week. Tiring of this demeaning work where she was treated more like a slave than a person who was being paid to work, she eventually left to take a job on a farming property in country Victoria near Ballan. It was domestic work she did there, but at least she was treated with some respect. She stayed there a couple of years before rejoining her older sister back in Melbourne.

I found all this out that night after we met under the clocks at Flinders street station. I came into town by train from Williamstown, and that seemed to be the best place to meet. It seemed that everybody used to meet there. While I was standing under the clocks waiting, I watched the man with the long pole changing the times of the train arrivals and departures. I wondered if it was the same man I had spoken to the day my compatriots and I had come in by train from Port Melbourne.

I had no more time to wonder because at that moment I spotted Mary crossing the street and waving to attract my attention.

She had on a beige suit with a cream scarf loosely tossed around her neck, and she wore this dark brown hat with a bow in the front with a tiny corsage of silk flowers tucked behind it.

I'll always remember that because she gave me a small photograph she had taken in one of those automatic photo booths.

"I took this on the way in," she said when she handed it to me. "I thought you might like it so you would remember what I looked like the first night we went out together."

As if I would ever forget!

There were four photographs on a strip, and you could see how self-conscious she was while the machine flashed and took each photo, not knowing where to look, whether to frown or smile.

By the fourth flash she had relaxed and appeared quite natural. This was the photo she gave me.

"Where are we going?" she asked.

I hadn't thought about that, I had been nervous enough just thinking about meeting her.

"Why don't we just walk along the street and if we see a place that we fancy, we'll go in there?" I suggested.

So that's what we did, and little by little I relaxed as I listened to her chat about her early life in Cobar, and the hard times she'd had after coming to Melbourne. Her life had been similar to mine in many respects, and I could understandd her drive, her ambitions.

We ended up in a Greek restaurant in Lonsdale street and I have no idea what we ate. We were both so engaged with each other's stories.

"Teach me something in Greek, she asked over desert. I'd love to be able to speak it."

"Ti kanis?"

"What's that?"

"How are you?"

"I'm good thanks."

"Kala efharisto. That's the answer. Now you say it."

She did, and her accent wasn't bad either.

"What's this desert I'm eating? It's absolutely delicious."

"That is called Ghalaktobouriko."

She repeated that a number of times, and again her accent was near perfect. At this rate it wouldn't take her long to learn.

Three months and I'd bet she would be fluent. She seemed to have a talent for reproducing the sounds of the language quite accurately after only listening to it a couple of times.

And so the night passed rapidly until I remembered I had to get up early to open the shop in the morning. We promised to meet again the next night to go to a picture show. She wouldn't let me take her home, telling me that I would find her place a bit of a slum.

She would go by tram. The only thing she would let me do was to escort her to the nearest tram stop.

As I watched the tram going up Collins Street she waved to me from the window.

***

Spiro and Mary in Collins Street

***

We went out several times to the picture shows, Mary and I, and we enjoyed each other's company.

We had a lot of things in common; she had been thirteen, the same as I was when she first started working. She had had a hard life too, yet she hadn't lost her sense of humour. She was fun to be with. Every time we met at George's cafe I could see him shaking his head as if to admonish me, but he never said anything.

Sometimes when I had lots of extra work and couldn't go into town I would ask a friend whom I trusted. Nick Kollas who had come out to Australia with me on the same ship, to keep an eye on Mary. It's not that I didn't trust her, I just didn't want anything awful to happen to her. I liked her. She used to meet her sister at George's cafe and after her sister finished work they often went to a picture show together.

I think my friend took his task too seriously; he followed them everywhere. Mary complained almost jokingly that every time she turned around Nick was there, smiling and waving. He always called out: "Hello Mary."

'The only way to be rid of him," she said, "was to go into the ladies' toilet. If we stayed in there long enough he would be gone when we came out."

"He means well," I started to explain.

"Don't worry about it. I just think it's funny, that's all."

I told Nick to stop following her after that and we never mentioned it again.

Finally I got up enough nerve to ask Mary if she was interested in working with me at the shop.

She had taken a job in the little milk bar that was situated at the start of Station Pier in port Melbourne. She made sandwiches, cups of tea and coffee, sold ice-creams and lollies. It was a rough area as there were lots of sailors and wharfies hanging around. They were often drunk because there were several pubs close to the pier which were always packed with shift workers.

She liked the idea of working with me and didn't hesitate to say yes. In no time she was running the shop like an expert. She got to know all the regular customers by their names and would chat with them and make then welcome whenever they came into the shop.

It wasn't long before we realised that we were in love and should get married; only there was a problem.

Although I had not seen my wife for many years, and no longer considered myself married to her once I had found out she was running around with another man, legally we were still married.

To marry Mary would mean I was committing bigamy. As far as divorce was concerned, the Greek Orthodox Church was like the Catholic Church: it was not permitted.

I tried everything over several years to get a divorce, but it was only when I could prove that my wife in Albania was living with another man that I could get the Church over there to annul that marriage.

As soon as that became official Mary and I went around to the registry office in Melbourne and we were married.

At least we thought we were.

It was not until years later, after three of our children had been born, that we found out, due to the confusion of dates about the arrival of the official annulment documents, we had not been legally married after all.

Did that mean our three children were illegitimate?

They all had my family name. We immediately went back to the Registry office and got married again.

Now it was all official and we had all the papers to prove it.

***

Once we had moved to 11 Douglas Parade the business became so brisk we had to buy another press and employ a couple of shop girls. We decided to bring Mary's brother Eddie over from Adelaide so he could work with us. I taught him how to press clothes and he became very good at it.

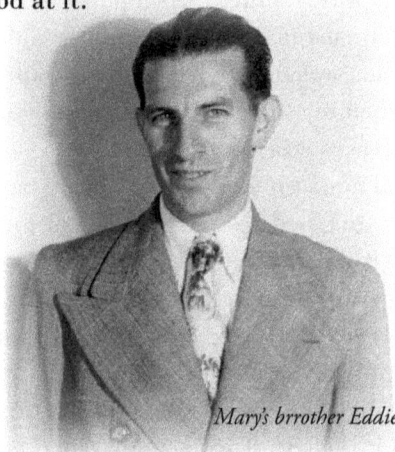

Mary's brrother Eddie

Things were really going well and even this shop seemed too small. When a house further down the road at 19 Douglas Parade went on sale we decided to buy it and build a larger shop in front. Between that house and our shop at number 11 was a large two story house set back on a huge block where a dentist, Dr Parker, lived and had a surgery. And on the other side of the house we were looking at was another huge block with a house and a doctor's surgery. Beyond that, on the next corner was a funeral parlour.

I knew it was a gamble because there were no other shops on our side of the street after number 11. There were plenty of shops on the other side. The Estate agent of course assured us that it wouldn't be long before our side developed.

"Business is moving up this way," he said with absolute certainty. "This will be the main business street in the future, not Nelson Place. You watch, in a few years Douglas Parade will be all shops."

At the moment we were renting a house around in Electra Street, only a short walk from the shop. We figured that if we could live behind the shop we could save paying rent, and we could build a small factory in the yard behind the house where we could do all the work. The back yard was certainly big enough for that. And there was a lane at the back too so access to the factory part could be gained without coming through the front.

It seemed like a sound idea so we talked to our Bank Manager, borrowed the money, and went ahead and bought it.

***

Before we moved to the new shop we had built at 19 Douglas Parade Mary's brother went back to Adelaide where he took a job managing a large Dry Cleaning factory. That left us alone with only the shop girls to do all the work.

There was lots of work too. I had a contract with the Army to do uniforms, and because Williamstown was a seaport and the Navy had some training facilities nearby I also got lots of bell-bottom trousers and pleated tops. And this was apart from our regular work that came in over the counter. We were working twelve to sixteen hours a day with not a moment to spare in between working and sleeping.

In all this time I don't know how Mary managed to learn Greek but she did. She bought a book to explain the grammar, which she studied carefully night after night. Of course I helped her with the pronunciation, and whenever we went to a Greek party or club social night, she would mix in with the ladies so she could practice speaking. She became fluent in no time at all. She must have had a natural talent because she learnt Greek a lot quicker than I had learnt English in America.

***

19 Douglas Parade in the late 1950s.
It was later remodelled but as it shows shere it was virtually unchaged from when we first built it.
Only the interior changed. Originally we had the clothing racks and counters in a circle around the shop and all the presses unseen behind, but later we changed that and brought two of the presses into the shop so our customers could see how their garments being finished.

We weren't in the new shop very long when George received word that our mother had died.

I was stunned and extremely upset when he rang and told me.

No one ever wants to hear that their mother had passed away.

It was not that it was unexpected, she was elderly and no one lives forever, but it always comes as a shock to hear something like that.

Perhaps it was made worse by the realization that I could never see her, or talk to her again. It had been just over twelve years since she hugged me for the last time in our village before I got on the truck that took us down the mountains into Greece. As long as she had been alive there had always been the hope that I would be able to see her again. That hope was gone forever now, and there was nothing I could do about it.

Tears welled up in my eyes and I couldn't stop crying for some time. Every time I thought about her more tears appeard to run down my face.

But finally they stopped because there was another problem: my daughter Verga. She had been living with my Mother ever since my first wife had run off with another man. Since my father had died some years previously there was now no one to look after her. I would have to bring her out to Australia but I didn't know how to broach this subject with Mary. Would she resent a daughter she had never met being brought into our house? Or would she welcome her, a young teenager who couldn't speak any English?

I worried about it all night and couldn't sleep. Finally, in the morning I asked Mary what she thought.

"Of course she's welcome," Mary said. "I would love to meet her. And don't you worry; I'll have her speaking English in no time."

It was such a relief to hear that. Now there were letters to write, papers to organize, all the sort of stuff you have to do to bring someone to Australia as an immigrant. Mary helped to organise that. I sent the money over to my sister and her husband who were to arrange the passport and the ship's passage. As it turned out she would be travelling at the same time as couple of other people from my village so she would not be alone on a ship full of strangers.

As the time of arrival drew near I became increasing nervous, as well as excited. The last time I had seen her she was not much more than a baby.

Would I recognise her when she came off the ship? I had those photos George had brought with him so I thought I wouldn't have a problem there, but would she remember what I looked like?

Would she think I had deserted her and her mother, and resent having to come half way around the world to a strange place where even the language was different?

I would be a complete stranger to her, yet I was her father. How would she react?

Mary suggested I take George along because at least she would recognise him. She would have been almost five years old when George left to come to Australia. Up until he had left, she had probably seen him every day of her life. Of course she would remember him, but me, all she had seen of me was a couple of photographs George had recently sent over.

Verga standing beside my sister, about the time she left for Australia

Well, there was nothing to do now but wait. She was on her way and that was that.

***

Serie 037 N° 00280

LLOYD TRIESTINO

SOC. AN. DI NAVIGAZIONE — SEDE IN TRIESTE
CAPITALE SOCIALE L.300.000.000 INTERAMENTE VERSATO

3a/37/280

BIGLIETTO DI PASSAGGIO

Cabina 159 III Classe

Da Porto Said a Melbourne Nave Rome Linea australia

Partenza 18/8/37 Ore Sig ra Verga Litchen

Adulti UNO Ragazzi ///////// Bambini /////////

Prezzo di Passaggio prevv Atene N° 14041 £ 28.10.0

Supplementi

Tasse: IMBARCO e SBARCO, BAGAGLIO, DIVERSE

TIMBRO E FIRMA DELL'AGENTE

Porto Said 14 agosto 1937 xv°

L.P N° 12256 esente da scorta

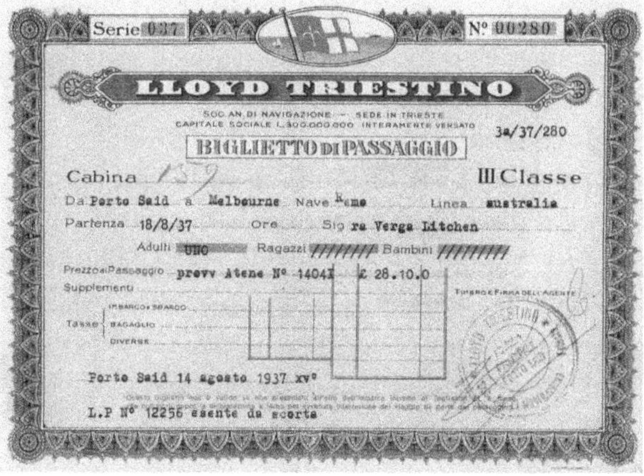

The ticket issued to Verga by LLoyd Triestino shipping line in 1937.

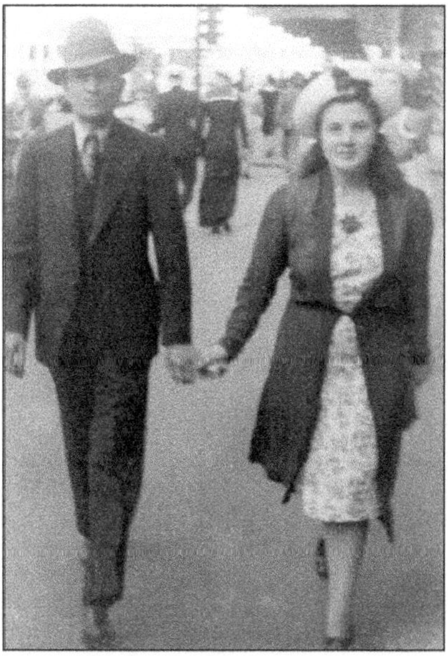

walking in the city with Verginia in 1946

* * *

It was a dull day when the ship arrived in September 1937.

I can't remember exactly which day it was, but it looked like it was going to rain. Typical bloody Melbourne weather. Whenever you want to do something important it always rains.

With our heavy overcoats and hats on we looked like a couple of gangsters as we walked up the gangplank.

Well of course Verga didn't recognise me... but she knew her Uncle George. She ran to him and threw her arms around him.

"Someone is happy to see me," he muttered into her ear.

She hugged him so tight he had to pry her arms loose so he could turn her around and introduce her to me.

"She's very strong," he said he said to me.

"Dad?" Her voice was full of uncertainty.

Was she as nervous as I felt?

* * *

"Hello Verginia, how was the trip? Did you have a good time?"

It sounded stupid but I couldn't think of anything else to say.

Verga just stared at me completely devoid of expression.

"Go on," George said. "Give your father a big hug."

He pushed her towards me. She hesitated, and then put her arms slowly around me. We hugged each other as strangers would. Then she turned back to George and started telling him all about what was happening in the home village. What her cousins, his sons and daughters, were doing. From time to time she would remember I was there and include me in the conversation, but it was really George she was talking to.

We went back to his cafe where we had some lunch. Gradually

she relaxed and after a while she became a little friendlier towards me, especially when she realised that everyone she was talking about was also known to me. Then we went around to a club in Exhibition Street run by a Macedonian friend. There were a lot of other people there that Verginia knew either by sight or by name, so she felt right at home.

Going home in a taxi afterwards I explained to her that she would meet a new mother, an Australian one, who could also speak Greek, and that she would be able to converse with her. I also told her that she was very nice, and that I was sure she would get on well with her.

It had been a long day and she seemed anxious, and that made me nervous again, now that we were getting close to Williamstown. Then we were home, and Mary was at the front door waiting for us.

I needn't have worried. Verginia ran up and hugged Mary as if she were someone well known to her whom she hadn't seen for years. They kissed each other on the cheeks and started chatting in Greek. I went into the kitchen and made a cup of coffee while Mary showed Verginia around the house, which room was for her, and where to put her things.

It was a fine homecoming, and I went to bed happy.

***

I suppose, later on in life you can look back over the things you have done and see all the mistakes you have made. It is easy then to say I should have done this instead of that, but at the time you can't know that, and you do what you think is best.

Verginia had been with us for six months, and with Mary's coaching, and the help of a couple of girlfriends, she was speaking quite good English.

She had not had much schooling in Albania and we thought

that the best thing for her would be to go to school. Verginia herself thought this was a good idea at first until she realized the school she was to be going to was a boarding school.

We had found this Catholic girls school in Windsor, and it was a wonderful school. They didn't mind that Verginia was a Greek Orthodox, and they had an excellent program for teaching older girls who had not had much formal education. It was the perfect place for her, so we thought.

We tried to tell her that she had to stay out there, but that she could come home at weekends, but she refused to understand.

We had all kinds of arguments to get her to stay there and she was such a problem for the Nuns.

Looking back now, I can see that she was convinced that we didn't want her; that we wanted to get rid of her and that was the reason we sent her there. She also believed that I had deserted her and her mother in the first place, something she could never forget, and here I was trying to do it again.

She never came out and said anything like that directly, but now I'm sure that at that time it was what she felt. She didn't think she could trust us any more. So she rebelled and absolutely refused to go to the school after the first few weeks.

***

Verginia (left) and two friends

***

I was at my wit's end with Verginia. She liked hairdressing and was good at it. She sometimes did Mary's hair and she did a really good job too. So I spoke to some people I knew who had a salon. They were willing to take her on as an apprentice, but suddenly she was no longer interested.

She didn't want me arranging anything for her.

"It's a good trade," I tried to tell her. "And one day you'll own your own business. You can make a lot of money as a hairdresser."

"I'm not interested in hairdressing," she said.

"Well what are you interested in?"

"I don't know. Why don't you leave me alone and stop pestering me?"

She turned around and stormed out of the room.

Neither Mary nor I had any idea of what we could do.

No matter what I did, it was wrong.

Here was a girl who was intelligent, though she had hardly any education in Greek, and none at all in English, yet she had managed to learn English in less than six months. So there was no doubting the fact she was intelligent. If she set her mind to do something she could do it, no trouble at all. But the problem was she had no idea of what she wanted to do.

She was stubborn and the more I tried to help her the more she rejected me.

What could I do with someone who had no ambition to do anything?

***

Verginia had a wonderful singing voice, strong and powerful, so we took her to see a teacher called Madame Filipini who told us that she also had a terrific range and would make a wonderful singer. So we arranged for lessons. I also bought a piano. She was to learn the piano as well since this would help with her singing and the ability to read music was neccessary to be a good singer.

Both Mary and I were happy because at last we thought we had found something Verginia seemed to be interested in.

We paid for the lessons in advance for the first term.

Verga seemed so happy at first but suddenly after the third lesson she refused to go back again.

She wouldn't explain and I got so angry with her that I threatened to send her back to Albania. That was a mistake because she out of the house and disappeared. She never came home that night and we sat up all night worrying about where she might have gone.

The next day a lady we knew, one of our customers, came into the shop and told us that Verginia had come to their place and was staying with her daughter.

"I don't mind her staying with us if you don't mind," she told us. "She gets on well with my daughter. I just thought you should know where she was so you wouldn't worry too much."

Mary explained what had happened and the reasons behind Verga's rebelliousness and the lady was very understanding. I told her I would pay for Verginia's keep, but she refused to take any money.

After a few weeks Verginia came home again, and we never said anything about the piano or singing lessons. Mary took a couple of lessons on the piano, since we had paid for them, and that was the only time the piano got used until that crazy Czechoslovakian came to live with us.

***

He was Jewish, from Czechoslovakia, and we met him at a ball in the Odd Fellows Hall at the top of La Trobe Street. He was playing Gypsy music on a violin and everybody loved it. He was such a fantastic player. He could make that violin sing songs, almost as if it had a human voice. He could play it so soft and mellow it would bring tears to your eyes. I had never heard anything like it before.

I hummed a Greek song to him and he started to play it. It was like he had known it for years.

"How can you do that?" I asked.

"How does a cat Purr?" he said. "Does the cat think about it? No, it just does it. And that's what I do. You hum the melody, and I play it."

"You must be a genius."

He smiled, and shook his head. "No, but I was smart enough to get out of Czechoslovakia. I went to England, but everyone I knew there was coming here, to Australia. So I came too."

"This is a good country for people like us," I told him.

"Yes. Excuse me, I have to go and entertain at another table."

A few seconds later he was playing an amazing version of the Flight of the Bumble Bee.

"We should get him to come home one day," Mary suggested. "You could hum some songs and he could write them down for us. Maybe he could even teach you how to play the violin."

***

There was a lot of talk about the coming war in Europe, and although I couldn't imagine that it was likely to happen, everyone else I knew seemed convinced that it was inevitable. Had they forgotten what had happened only twenty or so years earlier?

I refused to think about it. I had other problems. Verginia had run away again, but we knew where she was staying, so I suppose that was okay. I wish I knew how to settle her down. I kept thinking I had made some awful mistake, although I had no idea what it might have been.

One day an officer from the Army base in Williamstown approached me to see if I would contract to do the cleaning of their uniforms and I said yes. I never knocked back any work that came along, even if it meant staying up late at night to do it. Times had recently been tough and people didn't get their cleaning done as often as they once did so taking on a contract with the Army was a good idea.

It was hard to get the white spirit we used for the cleaning, all petroleum products were in short supply or were rationed, which finally convinced me that the war everyone talked about really was going to happen, but once I took on the Army contract I became exempt from the rationing and had no trouble getting all the white spirit I needed.

Then right in the midst of all this doom and gloom about the coming war in Europe Mary fell pregnant, and both of us were excited at the prospect of our first child.

***

One day a compatriot came to see me in the shop.

None of my friends ever came to the shop because Williamstown was so far away from where they tended to congregate in Carlton or in Lonsdale Street, so it was a surprise to see him.

He seemed nervous and when I asked: "What are you doing here? What's wrong?" He started talking about the weather and that it was a lovely day for a trip, so he came to Williamstown to visit me.

"You're full of bullswool," I said. "Come on, let's go for a walk and you can tell me what you came here for."

We didn't say anything as we walked down Ferguson Street to The Strand where stood not far from one of the old cannons that pointed out into the harbour.

"It's nice here," he said.

I waited for him to say something else but he remianed silent.

"Let's go out onto the pier where we can get a better look at the yachts in the barbour."

We went out onto the Ferguson Street pier and looked across towards Port Melbourne. There were some passenger ships moored at Station pier, no doubt bringing more migrants. They all came to Port Melbourne, all the Greeks and Italians just like I had twenty six years earlier.

"I want to marry your daughter," my friend blurted out at last.

"What!"

It came as a shock to me.

I hadn't expected that. I thought he was going to tell me his mother had died, or that some terrible thing had happened to his relatives back in Epirus. But here he was asking to marry my daughter.

"Have you ever spoken to her?" I asked.

I was quite stunned at the unexpectedness of his request.

He mumbled no and continued to stare across the water towards Port melbourne.

I remained silent and waited for him to say something else.

"I can't ask my parents to act on my behalf," he started to explain, still without looking at me.

"No," I said before he could say anything else.

He turned and stared at me as if I had splapped him across the face.

"That's not the way things are done here." I said. "We are in a new country and that is not the custom."

I had been through an arranged marriage. I knew what it was like. I would not want my daughter to suffer marriage because her parents had decided that this was what she should do, as well as who she should do it with.

If she wanted to marry someone, it would have to be her choice, not mine.

"I have to get back to the shop," I told him and started to walk back along the pier towards the foreshore.

"Well, could you at least ask her?" He said as he ran to catch up to me.

He looked so downhearted, and so disappointed, that in order to cheer him up a little I said I would ask her.

***

"Not in a million years," Verginia snapped.

She glared at us as if we had said something despicable.

We were stunned at her vehemence.

"I would never marry anyone from that village" she yelled at us and immediately stormed off in a huff.

And that was the end of it.

We never mentioned marriage to her again.

***

At that time, just before the Second World War, everyone knew it was imminent so they acted a little crazy. Many believed the end of the world was coming, because it would be much worse than the First World War. They could not imagine what this one would be like so they decided to enjoy themselves as much as possible before it happened.

There were parties and dances. Some were farewell parties for young men who had joined up or were conscripted and were about to head off for their basic training. Many were just parties for the sake of having a good time.

We had that Czechoslovakian violinist staying with us for a few days while he wrote down a bunch of Greek songs that I hummed to him. As it turned out, he stayed for a lot longer than a few days. We couldn't get rid of him.

"He eats like as horse," Mary complained one day. "A whole packet of Weet Bix and two pints of milk every morning for breakfast. Not to mention six eggs, and half a dozen slices of bacon. Thank God he doesn't expect lunch and dinner as well."

"I suspect it's all a reaction to starving in Europe. He probably never got enough to eat there so he makes up for it here, where there's plenty."

"I don't care about that. We can't afford it, that's all."

"At least he doesn't ask you to prepare it."

"No, but he leaves the dishes for me to clean up."

I couldn't supress a smile. Who likes cleaning up dirty dishes?

That night there was a big party up the road, so he took the piano. Like it was no big deal. Sure, I'll just bring the piano and play a few songs for you.

It was an upright piano, and very heavy. It took two people, with a lot of huffing and puffing to bring it into the house when we bought it. And here was our Czechoslovakian friend, as casual as you like, pushing it down the sideway, and rolling it up the street as if it was nothing more than an old lady's shopping trolley. He took that piano half a mile up the street to the house where the party was.

And when he played, he was like a madman, a genius. He would attack the piano as if it was something alive and huge that needed to be tamed, brought under control. He played one of his favourite pieces , the Flight of the Bumble Bee, so fast his fingers were a blur, and the notes so blended together you could almost imaging he was playing it on the violin, which he usually did, instead of the piano. At the same time as he played it he sang the sounds of bees buzzing and had everyone enthralled.

No wonder he needed to eat so much. He used up more energy than any six people put together that I could name.

He loved horse riding too, and after eventually moving out of our house (I'm sure Mary was instrumental in this) he lived with a lady friend down near the beach. He was a bit of a free loader but nice nonetheless. We often saw him and his companion, dressed immaculately in British riding costumes galloping furiously along the back beach on horses hired from one of the local stables.

Sometime he would gallop down Douglas Parade and doff his cap as he passed the shop if he saw Mary or me in there. For all his idiosyncrasies, he was a very likeable person.

When the war actually started, he disappeared and I never

saw him until many years later. He was living in Elwood, a much subdued man, teaching piano and violin to anyone who wanted to learn. Seven or so years later I took my first born son to him for violin lessons.

John with his violin teacher who always dressed for a lesson in his best evening suit and bow tie as if he was giving a performance at a concert...

***

My first son was born on April the fourth, during the first year of the Second World War, and Verginia who was now eighteen suddenly seemed to settle down.

She loved her little brother and wanted to hold him and take him for walks. She was a big help because Mary and I had so much work, what with the Army contracts and the Navy work coming in all the time that we had to work overtime just about every day.

Not long after Mary fell pregnant again and another daughter came along eighteen months later. The fighting in Europe was well under way by then.

Verginia taking her very much younger brother and sister for a walk one winter morning at the Williamstown Gardens. circa 1943. This was after she came back from Bright.

***

It was about this time that Verginia came home one day with a Greek lady and she introduced her to us. This lady said that her brother was interested in marrying Verginia and would it be all right if she brought him over one night to meet us.

You could have knocked me over with a feather.

Both Mary and I didn't know what to say.

The lady was obviously waiting for me to say something so I blurted out: "Well of course it would be all right. But, I will not arrange a marriage.' I was adamant about this. "If Verginia likes your brother and wants to marry him, if the choice is hers, then it is okay."

By the way Verginia fussed about, blushing and being very nice, we knew she liked this lady's brother and that everything would be fine.

I looked at Mary and she nodded.

"Bring him over," I told her. "We would love to meet him."

I made it very clear to Verginia after the woman had left that Mary and I would not force her into anything she did not want to do.

"If you really want to get engaged and married then it's your decision," I told her, "and I will go along with it."

We certainly didn't want a repeat of the problems we had the last time a suggestion of marriage came up.

"But if you don't like the man, all you have to do is tell us, and that will be the end of it."

How she met this man and his family was a mystery. They came from Euroa in central Victoria and as far as we knew Verginia had never been there before she met George, so she must have met him in Melbourne. But she didn't say anything about this and we decided we wouldn't ask. We could see she was happy, and that was all that really mattered.

George with his horse and his wagon in Euroa

When George came over to meet us it was obvious that Verginia liked him a lot. We liked him too. He was pleasant and respectful, and a good hard worker. A little older than we had imagined but he was a good choice. We welcomed him into our family with a big engagement party at my Brother George's restaurant.

This was a different restaurant than the one we had started together after George had come to Australia. This one was in Russell Street and he served three course meals for a shilling.

When he closed for the night the engagement party began. A Greek Priest made a speech, blessing the couple to be engaged and they exchanged rings. All the tables were shifted to the sides so there was space for dancing. The night was filled with Epirotic music from our side of the family and Macedonian music from George's side. We had a great time. Everybody danced, and lots of beer was consumed. There were tears in many eyes from time to time as the music brought back memories of the old country, and of people left behind. I felt a hint of sadness over what had happened back in our village, but apart from that it was a wonderful night.

Three months later she was married.

We had the reception at the Odd Fellows Hall in La Trobe Street. It was a big wedding with everyone from my village who was in Australia attending. Of course it was the same on my new son in law George's side. Everyone in Australia from his part of Greece also attended. There must have been a couple of hundred people in all, counting the children who had a fantastic time rushing about and sliding up and down the polished wooden floor in between the lines of dancers.

***

Verginia on her wedding day

***

Not long after the wedding Verginia moved with George to the country town of Bright which was near the snow country in the Victorian Alps. They bought a small milk-bar and sandwich shop business. But things were difficult during the war. There were shortages and rationing. and they simply couldn't get the supplies they needed nor did the locals have enough spare cash to support such a business.

There was a lot of panic when the Japanese attacked Sydney, sinking a ship moored at the docks right in the harbour. Two mini subs were sunk in the counter attack and the Australians finally realized that a war could take place here in their own country and that it was only a matter of time before the Japanese moved south to occupy the whole country.

It was suspected that a Japanese plane had flown over the Williamstown naval dockyards and then over Melbourne to reconnoitre possible attack sites and in their excitement the local gunners at the Williamstown rifle range later tried to shoot down an American plane thinking it was the Japanese one making a second flight over the same area.

Singapore had fallen. Our soldiers were in New Guinea trying to stop the Japanese advance, and small businesses all over the country closed down.

Verginia and George had to close their business in Bright and they moved back to Melbourne to live with us at the back of the shop in Williamstown.

My first grandson was born almost only a few months before my second son, that meant there were two families with four children between them, all sharing the one house.

There were also the girls working in the shop at the front, and myself and an assistant operating the factory and presses there during the day. There was nowhere for the children to play so it was not an ideal environment.

Houses were scarce but we didn't have enough money to buy one anyway, so we had no choice but to put up with being crowded together often getting on each other's nerves. Verginia had a second child, a daughter this time and that meant five children between us.

Eventually Verginia and George and their two children moved to Westgarth where they opened a milk bar.

I had to help them with money to get it started and Mary used to go over there every day to help them with making sandwiches and stuff like that.

My fourth child was on the way, and still we couldn't afford to move to a better house. It wasn't until two years after the end of the war when both my sons playing in the back of the factory accidentally set fire to a clothes bench finally convinced us that we had no choice but to live elsewhere if we wanted a decent place for the children to grow up in.

We managed to find a small house in Yarraville West, beside Stony Creek. Here there was rural atmosphere yet it was only a short drive from the shop and factory in Williamstown, or a ten minute drive to get in to the City centre.

Beyond the end of our street there were miles of open paddocks where the children could run free to play in, and a wonderful creek full of fish and wild birds. The air was clean and fresh with no smell of factories, and if you stood by the creek and closed your eyes you would swear you were far away in the country. It was a wonderful spot, and we loved it.

I knew then, that this was where I would stay for the rest of my life.

***

Here I am with John, Zara, and newly born Phillip at the back of the factory in Williamstown where there was nowhere for the children to play.

The house we bought in Yarraville West after I had the veranda converted into a bedroom for the two boys.

Mary with Virginia and John in 1943.

Getting ready for a family photo to be taken in front of George's cafe in Moe...early 1950s. From the left, Me (Spiro), John, Mary with Christine, George in the doorway, and one of the cafe staff with Zara. Phillip is probably next to Christine but is obscured by George's business partner making sure we were all lined up for the photo.

***

George moved too. He sold his café in the city and bought one in the country town of Warragul, an hour's drive out of Melbourne along the Prince's Highway. It was in the main street and he was there quite a few years before selling and moving further along the highway to Moe.

Although I missed George, it was nice that we had somewhere to go for a visit and a good opportunity to get the kids out of town during school holidays. We had to work, but the kids loved visiting Uncle George where they even helped out in the cafe, waiting on tables and serving behind the counter in the milk bar section. Each one of his country café's had a milk bar section in the front. The dining area was further in with the kitchen always at the rear.

When George had a falling out with his business partner In Moe they sold the café and his estranged partner moved to Morwell and started another café.

George moved right across the state to begin again in Maryborough which was renouned for its annual Scottish celebrations and the huge railway station tbat seemed too large for such a medium sized town. He never took on a business partner again and always worked alone after leaving Moe.

His last Café after Maryborough was in Hamilton, almost as far as you could get to the West from Melbourne while still being in Victoria.

When he retired he moved back to Melbourne and lived with his son Mick who had established his second barber shop in Lygon Street Carlton. Mick had remarried after his first wife Ruby died and he now had a son which he named after his father.

George lived happily in Carlton in his last years. Every day he walked to the Greek club we had first visited when we arrived in Melbourne back in 1924. He would spend most of the day there reading the newspapers, drinking coffee and chatting with our friends and compatriots, most of whom had retired and were doing the same thing.

***

When Verginia started losing the strength in her legs, at first the doctors said it was only nerves. After a while she couldn't walk and had to use a wheelchair.

"It's a curse," I heard her say once. "Always the legs…"

I thought she was referring to her eldest son, my first grandson Kerry, whose leg had been broken in a terrible accident with a motor cycle not far from our place in Yarraville, after which it didn't grow properly and as he grew it ended up shorter than his other one.

She had seen it happen as he had run across the road to go to the local milk bar. The motor cycle seemed to have come out of nowhere and smashed into Kerry.

But she was also remembering a much earlier incident when as a young girl she had been asked to mind her cousin's new baby, and was so nervous she had dropped the little thing. Both of the baby's legs had broken, and Verginia had been distraught.

And now finally, she believed, it was retribution that had struck her down, paralysing her legs.

The doctors couldn't find anything wrong no matter what tests they did or what treatment they gave her. She was convinced they wouldn't because it was nothing but a curse that was afflicting her. At first the doctors thought it was multiple sclerosis, but they did some tests and said it wasn't that. Maybe it was muscular dystrophy, but they weren't sure about that either. Not even the quacks she eventually turned to could help her. They buried her legs in cow shit and burnt incense and chanted all to no avail.

After a period of time she started losing the feeling in her arms.

The doctors were even more mystified and told George she should be in a nursing home, but both he and Verginia refused to consider that. As long as he was capable he would look after her.

He was a good man and I thought she was very luckly to have married him. He would lift her from the wheelchair. Dress her or undress her, bathe her, take her to the toilet, carry her back again, cook, look after the house; he did everything for her. Their children had all married and moved away so there was only the two of them in a big old house in Newport.

George was absolutely devoted to her. He was older than her by quite a few years and as strong as he was, looking after her full time became too much for him. He suffered a heart attack and had to be rushed to the emergency care at Western General Hospital.

He recovered and went home to continue looking after Verginia.

A year later he had a second heart attack from which he did not recover.

This devastated Verginia who had depended on him and she went into temporary care at the Williamstown Hospital until they could arrange for her to be moved to a nursing home or some other kind of hospital where she could be looked after.

They finally found another hospital but there was nothing anyone could do. Mentally Verginia was as alive as ever, but physically her body was dying, wasting away, paralysed.

The doctors never did know what was wrong with her.

After a while she refused to eat. She wanted to die. She willed herself to die.

Suffering the way she did must have been absolute torture, too much for any soul to bear. Who could blame her for wanting to die?

And sadly she did die, almost a year after her devoted husband.

She was buried beside him in the same cemetery.

***

A lovely picture of Verginia and George.

"What do you want another passport for?" the cheeky young man at the desk in the immigration department asked.

He had just looked up from my application form having seen my age written in as eighty eight.

" You're too old to travel."

He stated it with such authority that he made me angry. Who was he to decide whether I was too old or not to travel?

"What business of yours is it what my age is," I snapped at him. "Your job is to accept my application for a new passport, not to tell me I'm too old to travel."

"Sorry," he said.

Maybe he was not used to someone talking back to him. I had had experience with these minor officials before and they were all the same. I was not going to let him or any others like him dictate what I could or couldn't do.

"It's just that my old man is only sixty" he said by way of an explanation, "and he looks a lot older than you. He's not fit enough to travel anywhere. I just thought... you surprised me that's all."

I nodded but said nothing.

He glanced back down at the application on his desk.

"You're going to Albania, He said. Where's that?"

"It's in Europe, next to Greece."

"Ah," he said, probably none the wiser.

He stamped the application with a loud bang and told me it would take about two weeks, they would send the passport to me by post, and that I could get my injections upstairs if I wanted to do it now while I was here. He handed me the yellow booklet for the doctor to fill in the details of what vaccinations I needed.

Then it was Mary's turn, but no questions were asked of her.

***

This time we went via Greece. We didn't have to fly in from Skopje in Yugoslavia. Even though Greece had never declared peace officially with Albania and there was a lot less tension between them now, some commerce did take place. They were even allowing trips across the border so that Greek Albanians could visit their relatives in Northern Greece. Of course there was always the threat of imprisonment for those left behind if the visitors didn't return, so they weren't really free.

And the Albanian government had come to realize that you couldn't keep people ignorant for ever. They did know what was going on in the rest of Europe. They might have been able to keep people out but they couldn't keep out radio and television waves.

People could hear what was going on, and they could see it. And they wanted some of the luxuries they had been denied all these years.

There was a lot of unrest when we arrived, with government soldiers patrolling the streets in the larger cities. It was a bitterly cold winter and although the people had the apperance of freedom they were still abjectly poor, the poorest people in Europe and they knew it now, whereas before they didn't. They wanted a better life and were starting to become impatient.

The only thing that happened was that I got the worst dose of the flu that I had ever had. It was too cold to travel to my old village of Dervitsani so we stayed in Tirana with my nephew. When I looked out of the window of his flat and saw the people shivering in the cold queuing for food and staples, I was glad that I had left that second time and had never contemplated coming back to live.

"How could people let this happen?" I wanted ask my nephew.

"How could people be so gullible to let communism exist in such a harsh form that there was not even enough food for them to eat so they slowly starved?"

"How could they allow themselves to be ground into the earth, to be treated like slaves, yet made to believe that this was normal, that elsewhere in Europe it was even worse?"

"*How could their government accept the North Koreans or the Chinese of Mao Dze Dong as friends while pushing the rest of Europe, including Russia, away?*"

"*What was wrong with these people?*"

It would be a waste of time asking because he could not answer those questions.

He could not even imagine them being asked.

My flu got worse so they called in a doctor who said he thought I might have Pneumonia. He prescribed some antibiotics which my nephew was able to obtain only because he worked for the government and because he had a foreign visitor staying with him.

I tried to smile, to look better than I felt while someone took a picture of me in pyjamas and dressing gown after which I told Mary I didn't want to stay here any longer. I felt I was going to die, and if such was the case, I wanted to go home. I didn't want to die in Albania.

The doctor said I was too sick to travel, but I insisted so much, Mary agreed and we flew to Athens where we spent several days in a reasonable hotel, before getting the flight back to Australia. Even there, the hotel doctor didn't want me to travel, but I felt a lot better and wanted to go home.

"If I am going to die," and I really thought I was, "then I want to do it at home where I can say goodbye to my sons and daughters, and my grandchildren; my family."

That's what I told the doctor.

***

Putting on a brave face for the photo sitting beside George's youngest son who was almost the exact image of his eldest, Mick, the only one to have come out to Australia.

My passport photo for the second trip to Albania.

"I blame the English," the old man said while he waited for his freshly brewed coffee to cool slightly.

We were sitting in the kitchen having a turkish coffee as we often did on Sunday mornings.

"It was the English that gave Enver Hoxha the chance to take power."

He sipped water from a glass and then carefully allowed two drops to fall into his coffee to settle the grains.

"Hoxha was a communist, like Marshal Tito in Jugoslavia. When Fascist Italy invaded Albania in 1939 and absorbed it, Hoxha was the leader of a small group of bandits who fought against them. And then when Russia was invaded by Germany, which made them and the British allies, the British were under an obligation to help communist rebels. They supplied arms to Tito in Yugoslavia and Hoxha in Albania. They even sent advisers to help them fight against the Germans and the Italians."

He touched the edge of his coffee cup to check the temperature.

"After the war," he continued, "Yugoslavia and Albania were like brothers. People could move across that border without problems."

He started sipping his coffee, sighed, leaned back against the chair, "but not on the Greek side." He said this quite emphatically. "Greece and Albania were still at war and there were guards all along the border. No one crossed over, not unless they were smuggling something through

156

secret passes through the mountains like Christos did."

"When Tito had a falling out with Stalin, Hoxha who was a Stalinist closed that border also, isolating Albania completely."

He had finished his coffee and pushed the small cup aside.

"And that's the way it has stayed for forty years. No one allowed in or out. No news in, no news out. All the mail is censored."

"Those who protested or who tried to leave were sent to labour camps. They were worse than the Russians ever were. Whole families, including women and children, were forced to build these massive concrete pillboxes every couple of kilometres all along the border right around the whole country. The people were told the pillboxes were to keep the enemies of Albania out, to protect us from foreign invasion."

He slammed his coffee cup hard onto the table.

"Even when the army manned them and installed all the guns pointing inwards, not outwards, the people still believed them."

He had said all this before on numerous occasions but he still couldn't help getting very emotional whenever he spoke of it.

"They put them there to stop their own people from leaving. There were never any foreigners who wanted to take over Albania. It was all bullshit to keep people fearful and subjugated. Who would want to take over Albania? It is such an insignifigant place compared to any other country in Europe. It's the poorest country and has nothing that anyone would want. People eventually discovered that the world outside of Albania was vastly different, even in other communist countries. Everyone was so much better off than the poor Albanians."

He sighed. "And when Hoxha died in 1985 things had to change. You can't keep people's spirits suppressed forever."

"You know," he said as he placed the small coffee cup back on its saucer, "that Greece and Albania are still officially at war? ...After all these years!"

***

In 1953 I started getting terrible pains in my side. It turned out that I had stones in the kidney and needed an operation.

"You'll have to give up drinking Greek coffee," the doctor said.

"It's not Greek, it's Turkish."

"Whatever it is," the doctor said, "you'll have to give it up. It's too strong. And that goes for spinach and that other stuff you eat."

"Horta?"

"Yes, that. I'll give you a list of things you can and can't eat. And you have to stick to it after the operation."

I wasn't looking forward to an operation, a major one at that, but what could I do? The pain was excruciating.

My other major worry was what would I do about the business? Mary suggested we lease it to her brother Eddie. He had worked in a dry cleaning factory in Adelaide after initially learning the trade from us to begin with and it wouldn't take much to get him up to scratch regarding my business. That way I could have the operation, have time to recover, and have a complete break from Dry cleaning and still maintain a small income.

I had not had a holiday or any kind of a break since I started the business in 1928, so I thought it was a good idea.

I took five years off.

Eddie had a lease for those five years and I was determined to stay away and let him get on with it.

But I had to do something once I had recovered from the operation, so I became a Commissioner for taking Affidavits, and worked with a travel agent in the city, a personable young man from Epirus called george Bitsis, organizing immigration papers for Greeks wanting to migrate to Australia or who wanted to bring out other family members.

During that break Mary and I had another child, a boy, which came as a surprise to us. Christine had been our last child and she had been born twelve years earlier. This new addition certainly caught everyone's attention, not because he was born a blonde, unlike the others who had all been born with very dark hair, but simply because his birth was so unexpected.

I was glad I had time away from the dry cleaning business because it gave me a chance to play with my new little son Paul, something I could never do with any of my other children. I had always been too busy, which in hindsight I now regretted. But you can't change what has already gone, you can only make the best of whatever time you have at any given moment.

Towards the end of the five year lease, Eddie had let the dry cleaning business run down. He was a nice person, but had no idea of how to run a business. He liked to gamble but was smart enough to know that was fool's game, so he started a card game which he ran at the back of the factory. He took a commission on all winnings so he did quite well.

I didn't know about this until years later, but it was a big contributing factor in him letting the business run down.

Seeing all my hard work diminish, that things in the dsry cleaning were not going so well whatever the reasons were, at the end of the five years when the lease was due for renewal in July 1958, I decided not to continue the lease. I think Eddie was relieved when I told him and was quite happy to move on.

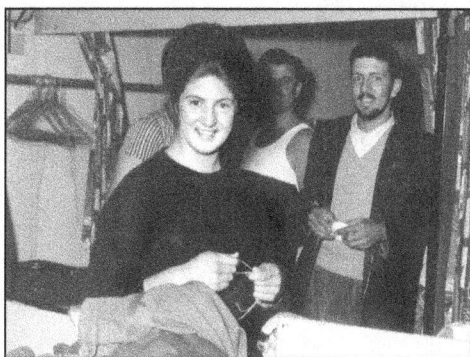

Zara and John at the dry cleaning factory in 1963

Both my sons John and Phillip as well as my two daughters Zara and Christine were old enough to come and work with me so I didn't hesitate to go back into the dry cleaning business, which now became a real family business, with the two girls helping in the shop, phillip running the factory at the back, while John handled collection and delivery to the various agents that we had established across the western suburbs out from Williamstown.

I stayed there until I retired at the age of seventy five.

***

We had to talk him into it.

The old man would never have retired otherwise. Even though he mostly came in later in the mornings and left earlier in the afternoons, he spent most of his time in the office doing the bookwork rather than the actual physical work of pressing or cleaning. He left that for Phillip and me and the rest of the staff. Sometimes he would chat with older loyal customers which he enjoyed immensely. We had a lot of people who came into our shop who had been coming there since very early days. Their children also came in as customers. This was typical of many businesses in Williamstown. They were multi generational family affairs as were their customers.

Once we had convinced him to retire, Phillip and I bought the business from him so it stayed in the family. We think he only agreed to sell the business if it was us who bought it. He wanted it to stay in the family.

He went to Europe in 1967 with Mum for the first time since he had come to Australia in 1924. It was her first trip overseas and she was excited about it. Dad was aprehensive, after having been in Australia for forty three years at that moment without ever leaving the country. He definitely wouldn't go on a ship. He had suffered severe sea sickness on all his long ship voyages and would never go anywhere by sea ever again.

"If I could go there on a train..." he often said, "I'd be off like a shot."

We had to convince him that he wouldn't get air sick on the plane, that in 1967 they were much better than what he had flown on back in 1925 when he went to Mildura.

"Don't you remember the commercials on TV?" We asked him. "The one where the man balances a cigarette on the tray in the new Comet 4 jetliner to show you there's no turbulence, and how smooth they are."

"But they don't make them anymore do they?"

"No, they had design problems but don't forget the first ones were produced in 1947 and started flying in 1952. They sorted out the problems, but this is 1967 and Qantas has much better planes now."

"All right," he said after a long pause while he thought about it, "but

If I get airsick, I'm getting off in Sydney and coming home."

"You can come home on a train from Sydney," we said.

"Exactly."

"You got air-sick forty years ago," we assured him. "You won't get air-sick in today's planes."

They were gone for three months and had a wonderful time. They could even joke about the primitiveness of Albania.

Then they went again in 1975, and once more to Europe but not Albania in 1987.

***

He looked like death warmed up when he got off the plane after that second trip to Greece and Albania.

He had refused a wheelchair; telling them the stewards on the plane: "I'm not an invalid." And while the anxious hostesses had hovered about him he slowly walked down into Customs at Tullamarine and they waved him through without even looking at his luggage.

We thought he looked like an Egyptian Mummy that had just been unwrapped after three thousand years. We didn't know what to say, we just got him home as quickly as possible.

"It's good to be home," he said, his voice an exhausted whisper.

We were fussing about trying to make sure he was comfortable and Mum told us to leave him be. We decided to go and leave them to settle in now that they were home.

Within a week he had recovered and was starting to put back on some of the weight he had lost while ill in Albania.

After a few weeks he was as good as new, considering his age.

***

When the Tall Ships arrived at the end of December 1988 as part of the celebrations for Australia's bicentenary we all went down to Station Pier to have a look at them as they came in.

They were magnificent.

Some of them were even as big as ocean liners. Never had we seen so many huge sailing ships in one spot at the one time. It made us think of what it must have been like 200 years eaarlier when similar ships brought out petty criminals and would be migrants to the new colonies of Victoria and New South Wales.

This was one of Melbourne's better days.

The sun burned out of a clear blue sky and a cool southerly breeze blew in off the bay so you didn't notice how hot it was.

Thousands of people shuffled along the pier gawking at the most beautiful sailing ships they had ever seen.

"It was just like this," the old man said, "the day we arrived on the Red Italia. Only the ships were all steam ships."

He pointed towards the end of the pier. "That's where we docked," he said. "There were people everywhere too, just like today, because a couple of ships had come in during the night and no one was allowed off until the morning when the Customs and Immigration people arrived to process everyone."

He turned to look towards the land and his eyes became hazy as he remembered the way Station Pier looked back in 1924 when he and his friends looked over the rail on the top deck and wondered if they would be allowed ashore. Those friends had all died over the years and now the old man was the only one from that group still alive.

A tear formed in the corner of his left eye and he quickly dabbed at it with a handkerchief.

"Come on," he said, "the wind is making my eyes water. Let's go home."

***

165

He had only just given up driving in November claiming that his eyes weren't so good anymore, and it would be better if he didn't drive. The truth is a month before that, just after coming back from Queensland he had probably had a mild heart attack as he took the car out, which caused him to clip the neighbour's fence. A whole section of fence fell over and he had to get someone to repair it. After the fence was fixed he drove the car up to the local shops once or twice then said his eyes weren't good enough so he was giving up driving. The car didn't have power steering and I think it was too much of a strain to manage a heavy car like his Ford Fairlane.

On the twelfth of December which was his name-day I shared coffee with him and took some photos. It had been fifteen years since I had taken a photo of him and me together, so I got my wife Monica to snap a few shots of us together. I also took a few shots when he thought I wasn't taking any notice of him.

***

...looking very happy on his name day 12th December 1988

*Our last photos together in the backyard at home
on Dad's name day...*

one of my favourite images

After coming home from spending the winter in Queensland the old man looked reasonably happy, yet sometimes when he thought no one was looking at him he got this wistful look, a kind of frail sadness. He also looked tired. On and off he had looked this way for the last few months.

Christine, who lives in Queensland, told us he had cried when he said goodbye to her at the end of September. He wanted her to come down to Melbourne for Christmas but she was unable to do so. He rang her after he came back and told her he would pay for her petrol to drive down, which she thought, was a little strange, but since she couldn't come she soon forgot about it.

She never thought this was strange at the time, but she now suspects as we all do, that he knew his time was nearing the end, and he wanted to say goodbye.

* * *

Although smiling he looked sad, as if he knew these were our last moments together

He was very happy with those of us who were there for Christmas dinner which was at my place. When he and Mum were preparing to go home he asked me "What are we doing for the New Year?"

"I don't know yet, probably nothing special, Why?"

"You never know," he almost whispered. "It might be my last."

"Come on Dad, you've been saying that for years..."

He just smiled.

Then Zara came in and hustled him and Mum off. She was driving them home.

The only thing we had planned for this New Year's Eve was to stroll along the strand to watch the early fireworks display, then have a couple of quiet drinks to see in the new year.

The tall ships had come in earlier in the day and it had been a truly spectacular sight as these magnificent huge sailing ships and a flotilla of yachts filled the harbour. We took Dad across to Port Melbourne earlier to see them moored alongside the pier he originally disembarked onto when he came here in 1924. There were hundreds of smaller yachts, all of them festooned with colourful flags tied up alongside the tall ships. It had been a beautiful day but the weather started to change for the worse as the evening progressed. The wind had become cold and blustery with the threat of rain.

Zara called and said Dad and Mum were going to be at their place in Williamstown for dinner and would we like to come along and join them.

We were just finishing dinner when a friend who lived on the Strand with a fabulous view across the harbour called and invited us to join him and other friends to watch the midnight fireworks display from his house.

We all wanted to go around, but Dad seemed reluctant.

"I'm not in a party mood," he mumbled.

But clearly Mum was. She always enjoyed a party. He agreed to go so he wouldn't spoil the night for her, and for the rest of us.

While we had been eating it had started to rain which ruined the night for those thousands who were lining the Strand waiting for the fireworks across the bay to begin. Quite a few gave up and left when the rain came pelting down.

It was raining quite heavily when we arrived at the house on the Strand and we had to park up a side street and run back. Zara with Dad and Mum parked in the house driveway and they only had to run a short distance to the front door, but with the rain coming down quite heavily they all got wet.

Dad looked very pale as he sat quietly on a sofa. He was breathing slowly as if trying to regain his breath.

That short run in the rain had been too much for him. Nobody knew until he told Mum later that apart from being short of breath, the run up the path to the front door, only 10 metres at the most, had caused his heart to palpitate and send pains through his chest.

No one noticed but he was barely able to stand when they got inside.

Luckily there was a sofa vacant and he sat down immediately. Everyone else stood around looking out through the huge glass windows across to the harbour where the fireworks were to take place.

After about ten minutes he brightened up when the host gave him a glass of champagne to sip. Just before midnight the rain stopped and the fireworks across the water went off with perhaps the most spectacular display ever seen in Melbourne up to that time.

By then Dad seemed fine and we were joking about how close we were to the end of the century, a mere twelve years to go. He was by all calculations 91 years old on his Name Day which had been three weeks earlier on 12th of December. Like most Epirotics of his era he never knew his birth date and so he celebrated birthdays on the day of his Patron Saint after whom he had been named. Saint Spyridon's day was the 12th of December. He could have been older than 91 by a couple of years, the only record which we had to determine age was a certificate issued after his Christening which took place on the 12th December 1898.

Earlier that month he had gone for his usual check up his doctor told him his heart was good, his blood pressure was good, cholesterol levels were down, and he was in full control of his faculties, in other words, considering his age he was in excellent health.

But he knew.

He said to me as we watched the fireworks after I joked about him only having to wait another 12 years to be able to say he had lived through a complete century and parts of the one before and after. "I won't be around to see another one." He gave me a sad smile and put his arm around me and hugged me briefly.

"You're always saying stuff like that," I said.

He squeezed me a bit tighter, but said nothing else.

In retrospect I think that was his way of saying goodbye to me.

***

Two nights after the fireworks display the phone rang and it was Mum. "Dad's just died," she blurted out. It was almost midnight on the 2nd of January 1989.

I had just gone to bed and had been half asleep when the phone rang. I was wide awake now. She wouldn't let me hang up; she had to tell me what happened.

As they were about to go to bed the Dad had felt sick. She wanted to call his doctor but he said he would be alright. He stood up and staggered, so she helped steady him as he had to go to the toilet.

Coming back out of the toilet he was having difficulty breathing and there was this tremendous pain in his chest. She sat him down in the kitchen and he leaned over the table. She rang emergency and they immediately put her through to the hospital where she described his symptoms to the doctor.

"I don't want to go to a hospital," the Dad tried to call out.

"An ambulance is on the way," the voice on the phone said.

"Don't let them take me to a hospital."

By the time Mum had put the phone down Dad had fallen back across the chair. He could hardly breathe, he was barely conscious.

Mum put two more chairs together and laid Dad across them. The only thing she could think of was to apply mouth to mouth resuscitation to keep him breathing. He was getting weaker all the time but he kept trying to breathe.

Finally the ambulance people arrived, and when Mum ran to open the door for them Dad's heart finally stopped beating. They gave him oxygen and a heart massage, but they could not revive him.

They made Mum sit down and one of them made her a cup of tea.

When she had calmed down she called me and while she was on the phone they moved Dad and laid him on his back on the couch in the lounge room. They covered him partially with a blanket and placed his arms crossed over his chest.

They waited until I arrived because they didn't want to leave Mum alone, which I thought was kind of them.

When I went in to say goodbye to Dad, he looked so relaxed laying there on the couch I couldn't believe that he was dead.

Surely he was only asleep, dreaming of all the things the future held for him when he was a young boy growing up in that wild mountainous region between Greece and Albania.

***

Mum and Dad in 1936

Before they left the paramedics explained that a doctor would have to come out to certify that he was dead, to make it official and he would issue a death certificate. After that we could call the Funeral Parlour to make the arrangements for burial. While we waited I called all the rest of the family including Christine in Queensland to let them know what had happened. One by one those who lived nearby came around and we spent the night drinking tea and coffee in the kitchen keeping Mum company while Dad lay at rest on the lounge in the other room.

It was about five in the morning and the sun was just coming up when the doctor arrived to examine Dad.

He wrote out the death certificate and time of death was recorded as 5 am 3rd of January 1989. Although he had died on the 2nd of January it wasn't official until the 3rd.

Mum called the Nelson Brothers Funeral Parlour in Williamstown and someone from them arrived an hour later with a hearse. They wheeled in a gurney and Dad was placed on that, carefully covered with a white sheet, and then with a degree of quiet solemnity he was taken out to the hearse.

The sun was shining brightly with the promise of a hot summer's day as the hearse drove away while we stood silently watching.

***

Mum and Dad on December 10th 1988

Dad's name day, 12th December 1988

LITCHEN. — On Jan. 3, Spiros
K. Dearly beloved husband of
Mary Eleanor, much loved
father of Virginia (dec.), John,
Zara, Phillip, Christine and
Paul, fond father-in-law of
George (dec.), Monica, Fred,
Chris, Wayne and Lynne.
Loved Grandpa of Kerry and
Sandra, Alexandra and Nicky
and Penny, Brian, David and
Dione, Melina and Anne and
Debbie, Michael and Tony.
Loved great grandfather
(Papou) of Melanie and
Andrew. Loved uncle of Anna
and Michael (dec.), great uncle
of George. Loved cousin of
Chris and Vasiliki of Narran-
derra, NSW.
Loved and remembered always
    Sadly missed by all
LITCHEN. — On Jan. 3, Spiros.
Loved brother-in-law of Jack
(Lofty), Bill (dec.) and Maria,
Betty and Dick (dec.), Eddy
and Thelma and families.
    Forever in our hearts

*Christine and Mum comforting each other while
the rest of us are lost in our own thoughts and
memories*

The last Farewell... January 6th 1989
R I P
Spiros Kiriakou Litsis -- Spiro Litchen

Most of the time Dad always dressed with a shirt and tie either wearing a suit or trousers and sports coat, but sometimes he wore a cardigan instead if he was feeling casual. As in those final images a few pages back it was rare to see him without a tie, or his hat. Here it is 1962 and he is relaxing in the back yard of the family home in Benbow Street Yarraville.

Re d' Italia. 430 feet Bow to Stern, Beam 52.7 feet.
Twin screw capable of 15 knots. She carried 120 second class passengers
and 1900 third class. On the run to Australia there were only third class
passengers. She was decommissioned in 1929 and scrapped.

Spiro with his brother George and George's only grandson in Australia. Altona early 1970s.

At an outing to Altona, George's eldest son who had accompanied him to Australia, Mick with his second wife Anna, and their son George, with Mary and Spiro at Altona, possibly early 1970s.

Spiro Litchen around 1980

In the middle of 1974 we had a family get-together, and this was one of the few occasions when all of my children and their wifes, husbands and children came to visit at the same time. At the end of this year I would have been in Australia for 50 years.

I thought we should have a photo taken in front of the house. The house had been renovated by this time into a beautiful brick veneer.

I think my proudest achievement above all is to be the father of such a large and wonderful family.

I am standing with Mary at the back while in front is Zara's husband Fred, My son Phillip and his wife Nijole, Monica and my son John, my daughter Christine holding her son Michael, my other daughter Zara, my youngest son Paul, and Christine's husband Morgan.

The three granchidren in front are Zara's son David, and Phillip's two girls Melina and Anne.

The same group appears in the backyard in the photo next page.

Underneath is Mary and myself with my youngest son Paul making fun of me.

It was a truly wonderful day with everyone together.

*My three sons together about 1959 or 1960
John, Paul and Phillip.*

...and fifty years later, the same three, John, Phillip, and Paul.

Fragments from a Life

Photo credits and acknowledgements:

Page 12, Halley's Comet photo taken by Professor Edwin Emerson Barnard at Yerkes Observatory, Williams Bay, Wisconsin, on 29th March 1910, and first published in the New York Times July 3rd, 1910.
Prior to this no photos had ever been taken of Halley's comet. That same year another much brighter comet passed close to the Earth and this one was visible during the day as well as night. People really did believe that the Earth was coming to an end with both these massive comts visble. Many bought gas masks so they would not be poisoned when the planet passed through the tails of the comet and umbrella sales were enormously popular with people hoping to protect themselves from falling particles and debris from the tail of the cocmet.
Halley's Comet passed the sun on the same side as the Earth's position in 1910 but when it returned in 1986 it passed the sun on the other side from where the Earth was in its orbit. In 2061 it will again pass the sun on the same side as the Earth and should be much more visible than it was in 1986.

page 66: Mid-ocean waves courtesy of Wolfram Dallwitz who travelled to Europe and back on the Ellinis and the Australis, two Greek ships that brought many migrants to Australia in the 1960s and 1970s while taking passengers to Europe for holidays. These ships acted as cruise ships to Europe, and from Europe back to Australia as migrant ships.

Page 70: Re d'Italia arriving in Melbourne 1924. Image courtesy of the Maritime Museum of Victoria. Used as a troop ship in the First World War, it was refitted in 1920 to carry about 2000 one class passengers, travelling regularly from the Italian port of Brindisi, to Perth, Adelaide, Melbourne, Sydney and Brisbane, as well as over to Buenos Aires in Argentina. The trip from Italy to Australia generally took about 12 weeks. The ship was decommissioned in 1929 and sold for scrap. A sister ship Regina d'Italia also made similar trips from Italy to Australia in the 1920s and 30s.
page 179: Re d'Italia images from Wikipedia

All other images are from the family collection of the author.

John Litchen

The Author - John Litchen

Originally from Melbourne (Australia), but now living on the Gold Coast, John was involved in skindiving for many years and lectured on Underwater Film making as well as writing articles for *Skin Diving in Australia and New Zealand*, which resulted in being author of the book *Cinematography Underwater*, (Oceans Enterprises), published in 1974.

He was also involved in music throughout the 1960's and 1970's, both with teaching and playing. His group 'The Afro Latin Percussion Ensemble' performed at seminars, Free Entertainment in the parks in Melbourne, at Latrobe University as well as the Victorian Percussion Society, in which John held a position on the committee from 1979 to 1981. Apart from helping to organize percussion workshops John also appeared as a fill in percussionist with the channel 9 orchestra on the Don Lane Show.

He is the author of *Convergence – Aspects of the Change* (Fiction from Zeuss), *Aikido–Basic and Intermediate Studies,* (Trafford, Canada, Yambu, Australia), *Attributes a Writer Needs* (Yambu), *Fragments from a Life* (Yambu), which in 2007 translated into Greek won the Agelidis Foundation's First prize for a Greek story, and a novel about people dealing with the consequences of global warming and rapid climate change, originally titled *and the waters prevailed* but now revised and retitled as *A Floating World* (Yambu). Another memoir *Fragments That Remain*, a companion volume to *Fragments from a Life*. In 2013 he published a revised edition of *Aikido - Basic and Intermediate Studies* as well as *Aikido - Beyond Questions often Asked*.

He is a teacher of Aikido as well as a student and holds a 4th Dan qualification in this art. *"One is always a student no matter what the level attained."*

A keen photographer, he has contributed to *Australian Photography*, *Neville Coleman's Underwater Geographic*, and *Blitz Martial Arts Magazine*.

John wrote a series of short memoirs for *The Metaphysical Review and for Tirra Lirra* Literary quarterly some of which became the basis for *Fragments that Remain*.

Writing about Aikido, he is the editor of *Aikido in Australia*, the official newsletter for Aiki-Kai Australia, and has contributed articles and photography to that journal as well as *Aikido Today* magazine in the USA, *Bujutsu International* in Australia, and several websites relating to Aikido.

John can be contacted at:
PO Box 3503, Robina Town Centre, Queensland, 4230.
jlitchen@bigpond.net.au

Fragments from a Life

ISBN 978-0-9804104-1-9

www.ingramcontent.com/pod-product-compliance
Lightning Source LLC
Chambersburg PA
CBHW022129080426
42734CB00006B/286